MOVING
WATERS

Kelley Susan Roark

Moving Waters

Printed in the U.S.A. and distributed by Moving Waters Press. For more information, contact kelleysroark@gmail.com.

ISBN-10:   0989330400
ISBN-13:   978-0-9893304-0-4

To those who try

DEDICATION

When we meet someone, we see him or her at the moment that is happening right now. We see the unkempt hair perhaps, or the shoes, the tired or the animated expression, and we make certain judgments. We attempt to see a person clearly, based upon the snapshot of life that is in front of us right now.

But no one really exists within a moment of time. Each of us is a composite of all that has come before. I once saw my parents like a sort of sad snapshot.... Two people who had "failed" in their mission to create a happy life for themselves. Two people who were often lost, frequently discouraged, and sometimes battered by life. When I was younger, in my confidence, I believed myself to be somewhat superior to them---to have a clearer direction, deeper insight. I saw myself as evolving and emerging from the confusion of their lives as a stronger, happier version of them, who knew enough to detach myself from their often misguided, unspoken life lessons.

Then I received the unique opportunity to hear about my mother's life from her perspective. For the first time in my life, I began to see the "big picture"---how she had really lived, what she had suffered, what she had loved and lost, what she had gained, and what she had learned.

And when that tale was told, I was left with a picture that exemplified the nobility of human life. We struggle, we love, we sometimes suffer, we advance sometimes after many setbacks, we are sometimes blind, and sometimes we obtain great insight. But most of all, we try.

If we are lucky, we live our lives with every ounce of pluck that we have left in us. We give all that we have to life, and then, when it is all depleted, when we are weak and on the floor, we pick ourselves up and we give more. That was the true story of my mother's life. She tried. She made every effort within her power to be the woman, the mother, the human being, that she wanted to be. She often felt herself a failure, but she never stopped trying.

I am both touched and saddened by her story. I wish that during that epic effort that was her life, I just once had held her in my young, strong arms, and congratulated her for a life well-lived.

Well, Mom. Here it is, 25 years later. This book is my tribute to you, my way of honoring the woman that you were, and the woman that you birthed within me. "Thank you" does not come close to adequately expressing my gratitude, so let me end with my most important message to you:

I love you.

And dedicated to P'oesay Apyan
And all of those whom he called brothers---
The human family.

FOREWARD

This story has two beginnings.

The first is in a small graveyard near Santa Fe, New Mexico. My daughter and I were travelling in the Southwest, giving ourselves a transition to returning to stateside living after four years in Costa Rica. We were driving along the highway in our rented car and felt drawn to stop in a little hamlet that we could see from the road. We turned, and entered a different world. This quiet little town appeared to have nobody home, and we wandered through a church courtyard and empty streets until we came upon a rusted gate, connected by a thread to its hinges, which led to an overgrown graveyard.

That was our invitation, and we spent the next hour wondering about the lives represented by those stones. We saw the ones that died early, the ones that lived long, the family plots. And then I came upon one stone that made me pause. This small stone, leaning a little with time, contained the words: "P'oesay Apyan," and under that, "Moving Waters." Something about the name moved *me*, and I stood for a while contemplating who this man was, and what his life might have meant. I put the name in my phone, as if he were one of my contacts, because I didn't want to forget that beautiful name, and I walked away with a profound thoughtfulness. Little did I realize that P'oesay would "contact" me nearly three years later.

So that is the first beginning.

The second beginning started much earlier, and in fact started with my first gasping, crying breath as I came out of my mother's womb, and was put in her arms for the first time. My mother was God to me for so many years. She was light and playful, profoundly sad, she painted glorious paintings and brought the farm animals into the living room at Christmas so that they could enjoy the warmth we were all experiencing. (I am pretty sure the ambience was lost on rabbits and chickens, though the cats and dogs loved it!) She encouraged and cajoled me, entertained me and irritated me with her endless stories. She taught me to revere nature, and to detest conformity. Sometimes she cried with a sadness I could only begin to understand over the cruelty that is an inevitable part of life. She adopted homeless vagabonds and lost kittens. She wrote stories, complained, raged and laughed. My mother was a bit of everything, and then she succumbed to mental illness when I was 14, and struggled with repeated and extended hospitalizations for the next 20 years, until she became the "shadow of her former self" that you so often read about in literature, and ultimately died of an intravenous overdose of lithium at the hands of an incompetent and well-meaning doctor at 65.

So in a sense, the real second beginning should be the beginning of my life, which I owe to my mother. But for the purposes of this tale, it would be best to fast-forward, to the time when my mother decided to contact me again, after her death. I know that it is unusual enough to have a conversation with your mother, 22 years after she has passed on. But even more surprising was what she came to say to me.

She wanted me to write a book. And she said that P'oesay Apyan was with her, and they wanted to write it together, and they had picked me for the job.

Hmm.

Well, since the mother who came to me was that dynamic, charismatic, and fun mother to whom it was impossible to say "no," here I am, with pen and paper, preparing to embark on what is possibly the strangest journey of my life to date.

I am about to be the scribe for a couple of dead people.

Well, without further ado, let's begin.

CHAPTER ONE:
BEGINNINGS

≈ ≈ ≈ ≈ ≈ ≈ ≈ ≈ ≈ ≈ ≈

Wilma's Story

I was a little girl once, though now technically I am a "ghost" or "spirit." I prefer the name "spirit." There are several things that surprise me about being a spirit. I am surprised at how things look at a distance, and to learn that I could have had that same "distance" when I was alive, but I tended to only see what was in front of my nose.

I was very surprised to discover that nearly all my pain, maybe all my pain, was self-imposed in my life on Earth. I "see" and remember everything that took place, and am surprised that all that had happened was interconnected.

When I was living those events, they had felt disjointed, but from the perspective of spirit, they actually were interwoven into a beautiful tapestry.

So my challenge now is how to explain all of this, from "beyond the veil." Where to start? Perhaps with childhood.

I had a disappointing childhood. I think many of you, too, have had disappointing childhoods, parents who didn't get you, problems that were too big for you to solve, and no one stepped forward. Here is my story.

My dad was a quiet man, and I barely remember that, because I was born in a small town called Saskatoon, Saskatchewan, in Canada, and my mother moved us from that small town to Michigan when I was 8, and I never saw my dad again. My brother got to visit him in the summers, but I never did, and he died when I was 18.

I was born in 1925, so when I was 8, we were in the height of the depression. My mom kept us going by taking in boarders, collecting the rents to live, then defaulting on the rents and moving to a different house when she got evicted and repeating the process. I lived in over 22 houses within a 3 mile radius in Lansing, Michigan, up until I graduated high school. I had no friends. People made fun of my shoes. I was pretty. Some girls were jealous, and spread rumors that I was "fast," which was code for "slut," and that slammed the door on any real connections in school. My mother was harsh, even mean, most of the time, but I was close to my brother and sister. One time I went on my bike into the country, and found a field of beautiful lilies. I filled my skirt with them and rode home with them balanced on the handle bars, and my mother allowed me to fill the bath with water and keep them in there until they yellowed. So it wasn't all bad. But there weren't many moments like that one.

I tried junior college for one year, and then took a job as a travelling saleswoman for sororities. I would go from one town to another like the Music Man, get to know people, start a sorority, and move on. I did that until I met my future husband, and then took my bundle of unfulfilled dreams into a marriage, and channeled them into my kids. I was a product of my generation. I did what was asked, or did my best to do that.

So what was your story? We all have them. Broken dreams, promises unfulfilled, moments of glory or joy. How do those stories weave into our tapestries?

~~~ ∫∫ ~~~

The journey of the soul has a starting point, but that point is long before a person begins a life on earth. When life is seen as these small events and relationships, it can appear very confusing. However, the point was never in what occurred, but in what was learned.

In the above story, what was significant? What really took place? I will tell Wilma's story now from the perspective of the soul.

A child was born, and was an open soul, reaching out for love. She reached out first to her parents, and they were not there. Her small soul drew in on itself, and she felt confused and bewildered by the fighting and chaos that surrounded her in her early childhood. Her father was alcoholic, and was himself saddened and disillusioned by his life. He was a poet, and a pretty good one, and felt he had so much to say that never got expressed or fully heard. His baby daughter felt that sadness and helplessness, and decided that she was like her dad, helpless and burdened by others who were more powerful, such as her mother. When her father had his children ripped from him, she understood that this would be her fate, too--to have her dreams shattered.

She was creative, too. She was a dreamer, and her mother hated that about her, and admired it at the same time, since her mother had been attracted to her father in an attempt to fill a hole within herself. She carried the same love-hate response to her relationship with her daughter, so the young child was alternately praised and berated, and something in her psychological makeup was irretrievably broken. She staggered through childhood, looking for answers, but most of all looking for the approval that she could never seem to find. Had she stayed with her father, hers would have been a very different life. He would have loved and nurtured her creativity, and transferred his dreams to his young and precocious daughter. But that was not the life that transpired, so instead, young Wilma learned that to dream is painful and that fulfilled dreams are unlikely. Still, she carried that spark of brilliance that made her mother envy and punish her so. The light was not extinguished by childhood, and Wilma eventually became an adult, with certain aspects of herself arrested in childhood. You might say she had gaping holes in her personality.

Now I will tell you Wilma's story, but this time from the perspective of Spirit.

A soul came to earth, to complete a process of perfection which is the Mission of every soul. This particular one wanted to learn to become empowered, to learn creative self-expression, and to cleanse itself of certain beliefs and experiences that took place in other lives before this one. She looked at her options, and knew that if she were to choose a life with few challenges, there may be few lessons. She decided to partner with a set of souls which would maximize her chance for learning.

She chose her father because she had known him for many lives, and knew that he would be an inspiration to her. He could nurture her creative talents, and make her believe in herself. She chose her mother because she knew that this soul would challenge her repeatedly, and this process would strengthen her inner beliefs. She chose her brother and sister to give her companionship and insight during the early challenges of this journey.

And what took place, on the level of spirit? Each soul had his or her own challenges to face. Her mother had chosen her father in order to develop this undeveloped creativity within herself, and to learn to be vulnerable, as he was. He in turn, was attracted to her backbone, and looked for her to give his life a concrete direction. On one level, each of these parents failed in their personal mission for self-development, and went their separate ways, failing to rise to the challenges that the environment created for them. This left Wilma with a break in her learning. She would now have to choose between development of her artistic skills and sensitivity, or development of her self-assurance through the constant challenges of her mother. Her spirit knew that she would always be artistic and creative, and since this was the stronger trait, she chose childhood with her mother, in order to strengthen her ability to think for herself and defend her positions with others. Her spirit chose the more difficult path, and the process of childhood was the battering of certain "weaknesses" out of her system, through the constant tests presented by her mother.

As a result of that childhood, Wilma grew up disillusioned, but with a sense of independence that enabled her to run far from her mother and everything she had ever known, take to the road, and define her own future. She decided that she and she alone would decide whom she married, where she lived, and what she did for a living. She was nearly fearless in these pursuits, because her soul had developed independence through the constant struggles with her mother, who became increasingly embittered with age. Because her mother was never there for her, she was forced to continue as an adult to make her own judgments and learn to trust herself more than anyone else in her life.

So as you can see, Wilma's childhood was a success from the perspective of spirit.

P'oesay Apyan:

Love. This is the most important lesson that human life brings us. I was raised in the great plains. My family was nomadic, and moved from place to place following the deer and the seasons. I was raised by the wind, by the tree mother, by the mountains, by our earth mother. My birth mother was loving and nursed and nurtured me as I learned from the tribe to revere my connection to my real Mother, the Earth. I felt her under me every day, supporting me as I grew up in my village. We stood together in a wide circle around our fire at night and sang to the sky mother, saw the star sisters above us, surrounding us, and we felt completely enveloped in the love of Mother.

I knew, when my birth mother succumbed to illness and died when I was 8 years old, that my life was still sustained by my earth Mother. I knew that the circle of my tribe was still intact, and that my little mother had returned to her Mother now, to continue the cycles of life and death. There was no fear in this knowledge. I understood my place within the Universe of Bigness and Beauty, and I was filled with excitement about what my life would hold. I knew that I would grow in strength in wisdom, as would all those around me. Since both my parents had passed from their earthly life, it fell upon the tribe to raise me, and I had many mothers and fathers. My life was very rich and blessed, and I learned to be a little bit of everyone who surrounded me. I took into myself the tribe spirit, and this eventually led me to become a great Chief of my people. I helped them through many challenges during our time together. We were eventually removed by the white men, and forced to move to reservations in territories that were unfamiliar to us. Life was difficult, and many of us succumbed to disease as a result of our broken hearts. But we also knew that our earth Mother was large and our sky mother and star sisters still surrounded us, and that our people would continue to rise. We moved on to the spirit world, and eventually some of us stayed in the spirit world, to help earth Mother heal the earth's people of their illness, in whatever ways we can.

This is my reason for writing this book.

~~~ ∫∫ ~~~

CHAPTER TWO:
THE GOOD YEARS

≈ ≈ ≈ ≈ ≈ ≈ ≈ ≈ ≈ ≈ ≈ ≈ ≈ ≈ ≈ ≈ ≈

Wilma' story:

It is my turn again, and now I get to tell you about the happy times in my life. This will take a bit longer, mostly because I have no desire to forget these years, and as you will find out, I am a storyteller.

Let's start with meeting Dick. I was in a train station bar in the middle of the day. And no, I was not ordering a drink. I was having coffee. This tall, reddish haired man with a wide smile and equally wide shoulders walked up to me with confidence. He was wearing a white shirt, suit pants (nice ones) and a tie that was loosened a little, as if it were his trademark, a way to look charming with the ladies. It worked.

He actually leaned over the bar in my direction, looked into my eyes, smiled with a twinkle, and said, "Can a gentleman buy the lady a drink?" I swear to God, he was that smooth, and it kind of turned me off that he was so confident. I immediately pulled out my card and gave it to him.

The card was printed on both sides. On one side, it said, "Don't go away mad," and on the back side, it said, "Just go away." He laughed so hard he got tears in his eyes, a big belly laugh that shook his whole body. It was that laugh that got me.

You need to picture me back then. I was thin, and had what they called an hourglass figure. I told you that I was pretty as a girl, but I didn't mention that I had actually won the East Lansing Beauty Pageant one year, and got to ride around on the back of a Cadillac convertible, wearing a banner and waving to the crowds. That was a high moment for me. I had wavy dark hair and green eyes, and my own impish grin. And I won't say that I was a clothes horse, but I had never had clothes as a kid, at least the kind anyone would want to be seen in. The sorority paid me well, and there was even an allowance for business suits, so I made the most of it, usually with matching hats and purses. What I am trying to say is that I turned heads. I was used to that. The card was a way to weed out the ones who were full of themselves and couldn't take a joke.

Dick passed with flying colors. We had the most amazing conversation I had ever had in my life. His layover was 4 hours, and mine was only 2, so he walked me to the train, and I loved the fact that he shook my hand to say goodbye. Most guys would have tried to steal a kiss, since they would never see me again anyway, but not Dick. Instead he gave me a boyish, strong handshake, which I liked, and got the address of my sister, which was the next place I would be landing where I could collect mail.

I didn't stop thinking about him for a week. Then when I called my sister a couple of weeks later, she told me that I had received a letter from someone named Roark, R. Roark. I was beside myself with excitement. We communicated like that for several months, meeting when out paths crossed (I think he may have shifted his route to make sure our paths crossed), exchanged long, newsy letters, and on the fourth "date," he proposed.

He did it in kind of a matter-of-fact way. He said, "Wilma, I really love to be with you, and I can only think of one way that I can spend more time with you. Will you marry me?" He had the engagement ring ready, and I was impressed that he knew what he wanted. He was the best option I had seen thus far (except a long ago boyfriend that I had lost contact with during the war), and I wasn't getting any younger. And he made me laugh. And best of all, he appreciated my sense of humor.

And so we were married. I want to tell you one more thing, because I think this is important to your understanding of Dick and me. He wrote me a long letter just after we were engaged. It was long and what I called "mushy," going on and on about how much he loved me and missed me. He said all these flowery things about how I had looked last time he had seen me, and how knowing me had changed his life. It was a real confession of love.

I was glad to receive it, but most of all I was amazed. I can't explain why, but I froze up inside. Somehow it was easier for me when it felt insecure, like he might disappear tomorrow. I wanted to believe in what he said, just take it in, but it made me feel so uncomfortable. No one had ever valued me like that, and I didn't know how to respond. So I responded with another newsy letter, and didn't talk about all that mushy stuff he had written.

The next time we saw each other was our wedding day. I wore a soft gray suit and a hat with a little veil. I would say I looked "smart," but not necessarily bridal. We were married by a "JP," a Justice of the Peace, in Salt Lake City, Utah, which was where our paths could most easily cross. Our witnesses were strangers, and we both were a little distant that day. I guess we didn't really know what to do. I think his people skills weren't much better than mine. We both knew how to do cagey, but not sincere.

On our way to our honeymoon, which was skiing in Jackson Hole, I tried to snuggle up to him in the car, looking at my wedding band, bright, new and shiny, and tried to take in that I was really married to such a great guy, and now we would have a family and live happily ever after. It seemed impossible, after all the pain of my childhood. I don't know what was going through his mind that afternoon, but I know that he stiffened up under me and kind of shrugged me away, with a gruff, "Come on, Wilma, I'm driving." I sat up confused and looked out the window, and one solitary tear squeaked out of my eye, but I tried to wipe it away quickly before he saw it. I didn't understand, but then we really didn't know each other, and I didn't know how to ask. I just knew this wasn't the way it was supposed to be, and somehow I think someone inside me shrugged off the whole experience, just said, "Oh well, what else could you expect," and then I got frozen inside for the rest of the trip. Skiing was fun, and we knew how to do casual just fine. I just figured that Dick didn't like doing intimate, so I locked that part of me away also.

Now I called these the good years, so I will explain that now. Dick and I had many goals in common, the most important being that we both wanted to have kids, and we wanted four kids. It was something that had astounded us both when we were dating. Neither knew how we had arrived at that number, but we both wanted four, not three, not five, and not six, but exactly four. We joked that maybe we couldn't count, and were trying for a half dozen. But four was what we wanted, and four was what we had, one right after another. He was five years older than me, and had been through the war, and I was 25 when we married, which in those days was almost an old maid, so we got right to it. Shannon was born in the first year, followed 2 years later by Mike, then 3 years after by Kelley, followed by Erin a year or so later.

And they were the love of my life. It turned out that I was made for babies! This was something I could do really well. All the babies were big, healthy, and happy. I nursed them all, and they were secure and content, quick-witted, fast learners, the apples of their teachers' eyes, all through childhood. They were adorable little towheads. Dick loved traveling and taking photos and movies, and we both loved to camp, so we had lovely movies of the kids in the early years, at Yellowstone or in British Columbia or Alberta or Colorado, next to lakes, seeing deer, fishing, running into ice cold water in our bathing suits. We used to have movie nights when the kids got older, and pull out the old reel to reel projector (it was new technology back then!) and reminisce over those wonderful trips.

The good years. After three years as a travelling salesman with IBM, Dick decided to take a job with the FBI. They were looking for business school graduates to become special agents, and he was a graduate of the University of Colorado, which is where he had landed after the war. Shannon was born during training in Washington, D.C., Mike in Minneapolis, Kelley in Minot, North Dakota, and Erin in Williston. He was moved every two years, with the last stint in Grand Forks, North Dakota, which is where the FBI train slowed and halted.

Dick had been assigned to the 1950s "Commie Squads," which were composed of FBI agents assigned to do the bidding of Joe McCarthy's House Committee on Un-American Activities, and he hated it. He was asked to investigate his fellow Americans on pretexts, and recognized that he and his cronies were contributing to the wrecking of careers, marriages, and even lives. He could not believe that the men at the top, and J. Edgar Hoover in particular, could possibly condone such activities, if they realized what was going on. So he decided to fly to J. Edgar and tell him personally what was happening.

This went off very badly, to say the least. When he returned to Grand Forks, he found himself under investigation. The Bureau said he was crazy, was paranoid, and put him in a mental hospital for two weeks for psychiatric evaluation. They took his gun away, though they did release him for duty again. But he came out a broken-spirited and disillusioned soldier of fortune, and just like that, the "Good Years" were over, and were followed by the complicated years.

Dick sat around the house moping, since they had put him on indefinite leave until they could figure out what to do with him.

I guess he felt like less of a man. I think no one had ever said "no" to Dick before. He didn't know how to handle rejection. He was always the best and the brightest. He had graduated at the top of his high school class. In the Air Force he had been a pilot, had even owned his own plane before the war, and had quickly risen to the rank of First Lieutenant. In college, he had been President of the Inter-fraternity Council of the University of Colorado, and had acquired his own plane again, working in his spare time in a sheet metal shop. (He used to go around campus with a dog that was half-wolf, named Pushka, and was a notorious ladies man, as evidenced by the photos he had kept.) After college, he got a job at IBM, and was in the "100% Club" in sales for 3 years running before he quit to join the FBI. Even in the FBI, he had received the prestigious post of being on the "Commie Squad," not yet knowing what it would mean.

So I think Dick crashed hard, and I crashed along with him. Remember that my own ego was pretty fragile, having had a critical mother and all that rejection in my childhood. When Dick fell silent, and I mean completely silent for days on end, I only knew it as one thing--the old familiar rejection. And I responded with depression.

I don't really know how the kids were cared for during that last year in Grand Forks. I had a baby of 2 and another of

4. Their older sister helped out a lot, I think. She was ten at the time, and a very old ten at that. Honestly, I don't remember that last year much. But I do know that Dick never went back to duty, and was released on a permanent disability check. I guess that is one way to get rid of unruly agents.

So now what? One thing was certain. I was going back to work. And without the FBI to hold us there, only a person with a lobotomy would choose to stay in North Dakota. So we hit the road-- something we both knew how to do. And we landed in Colorado.

It was a logical choice. After all, Dick knew it very well, having gone to 5 years of college there. He was an avid skier back then. One of our rendezvous had been in Colorado Springs while we were courting. We were headed for Colorado Springs when we stopped off in a little town called Loveland, to wash laundry and stretch our legs. We never ended up leaving. We found a cheap little 20 acre farm where the kids could grow up with country air, and these two city kids decided to learn how to become farmers.

Dick went back to construction work, and I got a job as a secretary. Isn't it funny how we go back to our roots. He had grown up in inner city Fort Worth, Texas, with a one-armed disabled railroad man as a father and a stay-at-home mom. I was raised by a single mom who was essentially a gypsy. And now we had moved out of our fine FBI homes and exchanged our bridge clubs for pick axes and weed whackers and barbed wire.

It is funny also that both Dick and I had always been very sociable people. We loved a good party, and the FBI had always afforded us a steady group of friends. He was a fraternity man, and I was a sorority woman. But when we landed in Loveland, neither of us had it in us to start over, to make friends again. There was too much to have to explain, too much uncomfortable history behind us. We became recluse, and just concentrated on making this tired, little farm work, and raising our four kids.

Thus began the complicated years.

~~~ ∫∫ ~~~

What happened to Wilma's soul during those early years of her marriage? Remember that Wilma had always been determined to become independent, to make up her own mind, to live her own life. She preferred to marry a man that her mother would never like, and Dick was every bit that man. In fact, her mother hated him. He was self-assured, and really didn't care what she thought. She thought he was cocky, in the few times they met, and he thought she was a bitter and man-hating old woman. There was no love lost between them, which only made Wilma more loyal to Dick.

Wilma, remember, had some development that had been arrested in childhood, and so while she wanted to show her independence, she was also still a child, and wanted someone to take care of her, and, most of all, approve of her. Dick promised to be that person, because he seemed to appreciate her quirky humor, and want to be around her. She thought she may have finally found someone who "got" her, and it didn't hurt that he looked good on her arm, and was so successful, compared to the family and environment she was raised in.

Wilma had her own soul contracts to fulfill, and since her father had not been able to feed her creativity, she needed another helper, and Dick appreciated her artistic talents. She no longer needed someone to challenge her independence, since she had proven that. But there were more lessons to learn, reasons that Dick and Wilma became a pair.

It was true that Dick was fun-loving, but he had also been scraping to make a living his entire life, and had lived at a very fast pace, with a lot of excitement--bomber planes and firing ranges, travel and arrests--and Wilma seemed to find fun wherever she was, without effort. She could make a story out of anything, and that kind of got him off the hook, about having to be "on" all the time, as the entertainer. He trusted her, and trust was something that was in short supply in his childhood. He trusted her right up until he told her that the FBI was following him, back in Grand Forks. But she didn't believe him, didn't believe *in* him, and he could never forgive her for that.

He always, irrationally, believed that if she had just believed in him during that crisis, he could have made it through without the withdrawal and the anti-depressants that they made him take. Dick had never done wrong, so he needed someone to blame and Wilma was the only one available. And she was used to taking blame for things that were not her fault, such as her childhood poverty, with her school chums. So she accepted the guilt that came to her, nurtured and fed it, and built it into her own neurosis. He didn't love her anymore because she wasn't lovable.

After the FBI, Dick ended what little physical relationship that they had together. Once they were settled in the farm, and built an addition to accommodate their growing family, he began to fall asleep regularly on the sofa, and when their eldest left home, he moved into a makeshift bedroom made out of a converted dining room.

One might say that these two partially grown adults were another casualty of the FBI's careless years in its campaign against American citizens.

What were their souls seeking?

Dick wanted, and needed desperately, to be able to see the world through the unique artistic eyes that Wilma provided. He had been able to see the world that way through a camera lens, but Wilma helped him to see it all the time. His soul needed to play, to challenge authority. He actually needed to be his own man, and Wilma, with all her insecurities, knew how to be her own woman. She had thrown off the shackles of her childhood and redefined herself. And he wanted some of that. The FBI was his last flailing attempt to stay within the grip of an authoritarian system. He had been raised by an authoritarian mother, whose only real attention to him as a child had been the backside of a hairbrush. He had gone from her to the military during a world war. He had conformed to the social norms of fraternity life perfectly, and been a "company man" with IBM, which was at that time the most "corporate" of the corporate, and traded that for being a "company man" with the FBI. He didn't just want to share his life with Wilma. He needed her desperately to show him that he could define himself, be his own man. He finally learned that lesson, and you could say he learned it at her expense, but that comes later.

So Wilma and Dick had a strong soul contract. He would validate her fragile ego, and she would teach him how to truly think for himself. It would take years for each of them to fulfill their end of the bargain, but they eventually would.

They escaped together, when they moved to Colorado. The question is: what were they escaping? And did the things they had run from end up following them to their new home?

The next chapter of this story will help to answer those questions.

~~~ ∬ ~~~

What transpired during these years on a spirit level? As you may have guessed, we come to this earth to learn lessons, to grow, to discover our true nature, our true essence. There are a few common experiences that tend to block those lessons. Fear is one of them, and blame and resentment are others.

What happened to Wilma and Dick on the ride to Jackson Hole? Each of them succumbed to fear. Their souls had chosen each other in order to learn intimacy, and to be able to learn from each other's strengths. But missing in both of their early years was training in emotional intimacy, and they could not clumsily make it through those early days and somehow find their way to intimacy. Due to the failings in their previous soul contracts, they now had some additional lessons to learn as adults, and they were just not ready for those lessons yet.

Wilma had learned to receive blame from her mother, who had always viewed herself as a victim of life, and of the decisions of Wilma's father. Resentment had been Wilma's "mother's milk" so to speak, and she was very familiar with it. Since she had been on the receiving end of her mother's ire for many years, it was "comfortable" and understandable for her to accept the unspoken blame that Dick leveled on her. She knew it was not her fault, but it was still easy to blame herself. So you see two souls who had a promising opportunity for learning together, blocking that communication due to their own childhood weaknesses, which you might refer to as "learned and inherited factors."

Dick knew what it felt like to be ignored and disregarded. He was never important enough to garner his mother's attention, and no one in his childhood had truly believed in him. He got his positive attention later, when he discovered he was good at school, and good at work. He received pins, and commendations, and sales awards, and participated in ceremonies, and this confirmed his value, and that others believed in him. When that approval disappeared, he needed desperately to find another source of approval, and his wife was it. When she withheld that approval in Grand Forks, in her own confusion and insecurity (never realizing that he could not see his value by himself, as she had learned to do), he felt this as the final nail in his coffin, and it made him feel more alone than he had ever felt in his life. He returned to that lonely, unloved child, and his wife returned to that child who was always falsely blamed and accused.

You could say that both Dick and Wilma went astray during these years, due to their fears and resentments. Opportunities were lost. Whereas the loss of the FBI position could have been viewed as a gateway to a brighter future, a "grand fork" in their joined life path, and in fact Dick could have affirmatively decided to quit the FBI before things got ugly, they were unable to see the opening door, because of the door that was obviously slamming shut in their faces.

You might say that these two souls in their middle years were beginning to regress. But remember that the story is not ended. They were still discovering themselves, still blindly succumbing to their disabilities.

P'oesay Apyan:

We watched the white men in the later years, when we were forced to live at their side. They came at will on our land, hunted, took anything of value to them, even our women at times. Some were respectful and others were not. We called them the ones without souls, because they seemed to move through their lives with words, but without real feeling. They moved too fast to see the birds fly or hear the rustle of the leaves in the wind. They were too busy speaking to listen.

We saw also that they failed to listen to each other. Many times I would see a white person with pain written plainly on his or her face, and no one seemed to notice. Each seemed locked into their own purposes, even in conversation, and they forgot to listen, not only to the words, but to all the things that have never been spoken, and do not need to be. This is why we believed that they lacked a soul, just as people sometimes think that animals lack souls. They were simply missing something that my people had. They lacked wisdom.

I was married. It was normal to be married, and we usually did it before we reached our twentieth year. We always married within our tribe, because those in our tribe knew our customs and our lifestyle. Occasionally strangers would come, and we would adopt them... perhaps outcasts from another tribe. But these circumstances were rare.

For me, choosing a wife was very easy. I looked at the women of my age who were available, considered my choice, and then I asked my elders what they thought I should do. In most cases, all would agree on the choice, and that was true for me in my marriage. We knew the spirits of each woman in the tribe very well, and the elders knew my spirit. It was easy to see which personalities, when paired, would bring the most peace. We knew we would learn from each other over our lives, but we would never be truly alone together, and thus we would never need to be "everything" for each other. We saw that the white men, in their families, lived in isolation from the tribe.

How can a person learn all that life has to teach, if he is near only one teacher? Each person has his or her own set of unique eyes, and no two sets of eyes are alike. How can we learn all there is to know, if we do not learn to see through the eyes of many others?

So I married to one of the women who shared my tribe. We continued to learn from our elders, our families, and our friends, as well as from each other. And we shared the sacred bond of sex with each other, which made us feel one with each other, one with Mother, one with the trees around us. We allowed ourselves to stay within the embrace of love for long hours, studying and knowing each other on the level of our souls. We used the windows of our eyes to see deeply and understand each other's pain and pleasure. This was our joy, and what made our union strong. This and the joy of bringing a small life into the world, which my wife and I did on five separate occasions.

We were very fortunate that only one of our children was lost, and four made it to adulthood and even had families of their own. Knowing that her spirit and mine had been joined to create those lives was an endless source of wonderment for both of us, and bonded us more surely to each other. We set upon teaching our children from young ages the lessons of our elders, and of the tribe, and since I became Chief of the Elders in my later years, I had the opportunity to give counsel to my sons many times over their lives. Their mother too was a Spirit Mother in our tribe, a position of honor, because she could speak for the souls of those who had left their human body. This was a great gift for many, to learn the thoughts of their elders after they had passed, or to solve the mystery of the disappearance of a member of the tribe.

Our one small daughter was lost to a disease which some white men referred to as the "pox." We were lucky that only three children in our tribe were lost to this disease. Some of our brothers from another tribe came and told us that the white man was giving away "poison blankets," and to be careful how we traded. We were beginning to trade when this message came to us. The elders immediately met, and decided that we could live without the white men's gifts, and we decided to move our camp for a season. When we returned to this hunting ground again to trade with the white men, we accepted only gold and silver in exchange for our pelts and wild grains.

But unfortunately, since I was already a chief at that time, I had been sent to bring back the samples of the white men's wares to my brothers. I had touched the poison blankets, and without my knowing it, the dark spirit transferred through me to my daughter, and she died soon after, that spring.

I was very fortunate that my wife and I lived to an old age, and were able to raise our sons to maturity. We never ceased to thank our Mother Spirit for having blessed us with so much prosperity in our lives. We learned to live each day with gratitude, and we learned that gratitude made it impossible to feel either fear or resentment. We knew that the white men thought us to be simple for not holding our anger or resenting our oppressors. They did not understand that anger and resentment are emotions that imprison those who feel them. We were far too filled with the experiences of each day to remember the day before. We held no room for fear or resentment in our lives.

~~~ ∫∫ ~~~

CHAPTER THREE:
CHILDREN

≈ ≈ ≈ ≈ ≈ ≈ ≈ ≈ ≈ ≈ ≈

Wilma's story:

We arrived in Colorado with an eagerness to start over, to find a life that reminded us not at all of the life we had just left. This farm was perfect for us. It was broken down and neglected, kind of like our broken souls, and as we fixed it up bit by bit, we found healing. We started to talk to each other, to plan again. Dick became an amateur draftsman, and drew up plans for a large living room addition with a big stone fireplace and paneled walls, and he built it to perfection. He put cedar siding on the outside of this poor little clapboard house, to match the walls of the addition, and stained it with a deep redwood stain, and I helped him paint the shutters white.

We installed new linoleum on some of the sloping floors of our little shack, and carpeted the others, except in our new living room, where the wood floor had a large oval rag rug in earth tones, which was beautiful. Dick was very good with his hands, just as he was good with the other things he had tried, and he was a very hard worker. I developed a new appreciation for him, and really began to love him more deeply, as I saw the love and the creativity that he put into all of his projects. He set up a workshop in the old garage, and began to accumulate tools. I think that this was probably a dream of his, to finally have the space to work and fix things. He started buying old cars with the idea of fixing them up, and they accumulated in the yards around us, one at a time, over the years. But I found that to be eccentric and endearing about him.

It turned out that Dick was far more eccentric than I had ever imagined. I thought that I had married a straight up company man, but it turned out that his "crazy" had just never had a chance to come out. In retrospect, he had always been a bit of an iconoclast, trying to make it into the straightjacket of the business and government world, but it had never suited him to be a "suit," you might say. He was more comfortable with his Pendleton wool shirts, jeans and work boots, driving to the hardware store with two dogs sticking their heads out of his van windows.

Fixing up what I called our "ramshackle farm" or "El Rancho Mañana" (the ranch tomorrow) was a project that took some years. We got all the kids involved, cutting down barbed wire and replacing it with rail fences. I started to paint, and painted a Pennsylvania Dutch symbol for good luck and prosperity, and we installed it on our big barn, which we converted from soft silver gray to bright red. We cleared weeds endlessly, cut down dead trees, and seeded our lawn and watered it like crazy, enduring mud until soft yellow green grass started poking itself up through the soil, in little delicate tendrils that almost made you want to cry to see them.

In fact, many things were growing in me during those years. I got the first job that I applied for, which was being a grocery clerk at the Derby Hill Market, only two fields away from our house, along a highway which was called "Lincoln Road" in this part of town. Since Dick had turned blue collar, I followed suit, and it was kind of liberating for me to no longer have to maintain appearances for anyone... not other agents, nor the prying eyes of their wives. I was someone new now. I was Wilma, the farm wife!

And the farm was the best thing that could have happened to our sad-eyed children. We got the oldest her own horse, which had always been a dream of hers, and she joined the "Sweetheart Riders," a "4H" club, and learned all about bridles and saddles and horse confirmation, and rode in parades. I saw her smile more, and even become bubbly. My son made friends with a boy in a farm across the highway, and learned to hunt rabbit, and took long walks with the dogs, looking up at the mountains in the distance and thinking "deep thoughts." My two youngest, who were only four and five when we moved to Colorado, were delighted by the steady stream of puppies, chicks, kittens, and bunnies that the farm provided. I was equally delighted, and experienced a kind of second childhood through them. You might even say that I experienced a first childhood, since this time I was able to enjoy all the luxuries of play without the punishing criticism of an overbearing mother.

I wanted my children to know only acceptance and approval, and I did my best to give them that. I praised everything they did. I encouraged them all to draw, and even paint. They threw themselves into projects like painting their own rooms, and I let them choose the colors and designs of their rooms. My own tastes began to change. When we finished the "addition," as it was named forever thereafter, we bought a beautiful old vintage upright piano with a warm tone, and all of us began to learn to play. I discovered that I could sing, and the kids and I used to stand around together and sing old show tunes, with sheet music I had picked up for a "song,' so to speak, at the local music store. My eldest two daughters actually took lessons long enough to learn classical pieces and do recitals, and I felt so proud and happy inside, in a way that they could never understand, having never known the darkness that was my childhood.

As I watched my children grow, saw their easy smiles, saw them actually have friends and slumber parties, took them on family picnics to the mountains for the 4th of July, bought them their first shiny new bikes and watched them wobble their way to assurance on our long dirt driveway in the blinding Colorado sun, I began to heal inside. I began to believe in life again, regained my old optimism and sense of humor. I laughed, a lot. I could feel that I had become the center of my children's lives, as a mother should be. I felt proud, really proud of myself. I knew I had done well, and even really well, with my life. I had rebuilt it from the ashes. We had done that together.

So my husband no longer slept with me, and was often still lost in his old world. He too was happy in his own fashion, tinkering with his toys, learning to irrigate, buying and driving a tractor, hauling bales of hay with his son, taking long drives and explores in the mountains with his children. We didn't talk to each other much, except about the practicalities of life, but at least I had a companion to raise my children with, which was far more than my mother'd had. I was Wilma Roark, wife and mother, and I was a success. I even got a job at the local Chamber of Commerce as a secretary, which evolved into a kind of office manager, in partnership with my boss, who loved my creativity. I would paint signs advertising Chamber events, decorate the counters on holidays, and there was an endless stream of businessmen coming in each day to entertain me with their stories. My life was really, really interesting.

What had looked like a retreat in disgrace had turned into a renaissance of sorts, for all of us. Life was full of surprises, and I began to love it with all the passion that I had kept locked inside my entire lifetime.

Dick, on the other hand, had not shared all of my experiences of revival. He had taken a couple of company jobs, which lasted a year or two each, even got back into a tie again a couple of times, and though we attempted going to company events and meeting his coworkers, our hearts were not in it anymore. We felt like "fish out of water" in that environment nowadays, and just wanted to retreat to the safety of our little farm. Besides, because of all that we had gone through, we were just different than them. Dick had been in several foreign countries and over 44 states in his traveling years, and minus the trip abroad, I wasn't far behind him. These were small town people, few of them college-educated, and we really had more in common with the local farmers than the corporate drones. I understood when Dick began to gravitate toward sheet metal work again, and ultimately took a job as a sheet metal foreman, traveling for a month or two at a time to complete jobs in other states. I even learned to irrigate in his absence, and the truth was that these short absences were a welcome relief for me, since he and I were not close. I had my kids, and they were endless entertainment. They were quirky and smart, playful, warm and creative. They brought me little mother's day gifts from school, and made me homemade gifts on my birthday, and ran up to me spontaneously and said, "I love you, Mom!" once in a while (except of course my son, when he hit his teens, and that was no longer "cool" to do).

The point is that I was happy and grateful for what I had. My life was complete, with or without Dick's attentions. I think he felt that he was a bit of a "fifth wheel" around the farm, more of a function than a participant. He didn't know how to interact with the kids. He bought them a couple of encyclopedia sets, and when our curious children came to him with a question about how something worked, he would bark, "Look it up!" and bury his head in his newspaper again. He wasn't all bad. I figured that this is what fathers did, having never really been raised by one.

I guess I didn't see the storms brewing on the horizon.

~~~ ∫∫ ~~~

From a soul perspective, what a welcome relief the farm brought this love-starved family. They had moved from the long winters and cloudy skies of North Dakota and a veritable "long winter" of disappointments, into the sunshine of a new day in Colorado. The relief was tangible. Each of them began to express his or her creativity, and as we promised, Wilma's creative expression had begun to rub off on Dick. He was learning to create his own environment, and to feel a master of his own destiny. The problem for Dick was that he did not really know what he wanted. In Colorado, he came to realize that he had spent most of his life seeking other people's approval, to make up for the deficit of attention in his childhood. For him, the absence of anyone at all to answer to was a little terrifying. He began to feel invisible, and it didn't help that his wife seemed to take to this new life like a duck to water.

He began to feel more and more isolated, from everyone, including himself. He spent long days in a sort of blankness, that had he recognized it, was in fact a depression, bought on by the ending of the long trauma of his years in the FBI. Because Wilma had never understood him, in his view, and had not believed in him, he wrongly assumed that she would not have been interested in hearing about his confusion over what had happened. He was a man, and he was not supposed to share weakness. In fact, Wilma would have been understanding and sympathetic, and understood far more than he realized. But those conversations never happened. His soul hurt, and because he suffered alone, the suffering was prolonged, and eventually intensified.

At first, he could throw himself into fixing up this old farm. But once the fences were in place, there were cars in the driveway, his workshop was full of tools, the horses grazed in the fields and he had found someone to plow and plant each season, once the addition was built on the house, and a fire was crackling in the fireplace, what was he needed for? They seemed fine without him. Once again, Dick had become invisible, and he had fallen yet again into the wounds of his early childhood. Would it ever end?

You have seen what happened to Wilma. She healed. She truly healed. She learned to love, to give, to appreciate life, including the people around her. She created strong bonds with her boss and her children. She even gave to the community, became a girl scout leader, joined a church, began to visit nursing homes to chat it up with the lonely old folks, and picked the worst home in town as her target, where an epileptic girl was put in a diaper and left on a blanket on a floor all day to writhe without stimulation. Wilma's big heart opened up to that girl and she would visit her weekly, smile and talk to her, tell her stories, and make her smile and feel important. Wilma, it turns out, was a giver, and with the fertile environment in which she now found herself, her soul began to grow into the beautiful being that it had always been. She fulfilled her early promise.

So as you can see, Dick was now on the road to finding his independence, and Wilma was on her way to acceptance and self-approval. So what happens next? A happy ending? Well, not in the conventional sense of the word, but certainly the lessons continued. These two were not finished "giving" life lessons to each other.

~~~ ∫∫ ~~~

On the level of spirit, hope had begun to grow in Wilma, and she began to want to feel a higher power, to understand a God who could deliver so much pain and yet so much love and pleasure. On a deeper level, she was now healed enough to move from crisis to a search for meaning. She now had the "what" of life, and was beginning, in the back of her mind, to wonder about the "why." Her soul was evolving, and as occurs with all souls, the time eventually came when she was able to step back from her own life and ask, "But why am I here, really? This is fun, it is beautiful, but why is it all happening?"

As a child, Wilma was in survival mode, and remember that she took many deficits into adulthood, causing her to remain in survival mode for many years past childhood. Not until Colorado had her life provided enough stability for her to stop and take a look around. That time was now approaching.

Dick, in his own private way, was approaching his own crisis in faith. He had been raised Baptist, and was well-indoctrinated in the idea of a punishing God, who knew all and usually did not approve of what he saw. His early adult years had been an escape from the guilt-ridden religion of his Texas childhood, and he was loath to return to those concepts, but they kept sneaking into his head again and again. He had an underlying feeling of worthlessness and invisibility that seemed to be intensifying with time. Couldn't this be because he was a sinner, and was in need of returning to Christ, and experiencing his salvation? He needed something to fill the hole inside. He had no friends. He could not talk to his wife, and did not know how to talk to his kids. Who did he have left, but that big and powerful, punishing Man Upstairs, who would be more than willing to tell him what to do?

Dick struggled with a return to God the way a man struggles with approaching quicksand after having been sucked in and nearly lost once before. He became obsessed with the idea of his sinfulness, and decided that his alienation was due to his distance from his Creator. A point came when he was at his lowest, and had even drunken himself into a stupor, alone in his lawn chair, tipping over from a sitting position and having to be pulled inside to bed by his distant wife. Something had to give, and on that fateful day, Dick turned his radio to a "fire and brimstone" preacher, and sat riveted on the toilet in his little farm bathroom, listening to a message that finally got through. Jesus loved him and wanted to save him, and so he prayed that day, and gave himself over to Christ.

On a spirit level, this was a step in the right direction. It would be years before he shared this conversion with his family, because Dick had now become a recluse. But privately, he had found a new purpose. He used a set of headphones, and listened to preachers exhort him all day long, even at work. He kept a Bible by his bed, and began his first halting attempts to find communication with his Creator. Yes, he was still lonely, and yes, he still worshipped a punishing God, but he had now found meaning in his empty life.

In the year or two before this conversion, Dick had taken to making short, exploratory journeys, to New Mexico mostly, but also to Wyoming, Montana, and Utah. He felt everything piling up inside, and without informing Wilma, he would simply disappear for a few days, and come back a bit refreshed. She understood that he needed these trips, and didn't really mind at first. The truth was that things were a bit easier without his dour presence. She didn't go so far as to encourage him, but she enjoyed the breaks. He returned a couple of times with drifters that he had found hitchhiking, and Wilma's instinct to help the wounded bird caused her to take them in and attempt to find them what they needed, whether it was a job, a meal, or a listening ear. Dick's trips had been motivated by his curiosity over the sightings of extra-terrestrials, mostly in the southwest, described by late night radio talk show hosts. He would go to these small towns where the sightings had occurred, sometimes with one of his children in tow, and use his investigative skills to get to the bottom of the alleged sightings. Secretly, he dreamed of creating a book that was a kind of expose on government cover-ups of extra-terrestrial contacts. He now had an underlying suspicion about all things government. He even suspected sometimes that the FBI was still keeping tabs on him. (He was on the right track perhaps with his ET ideas, just a few decades too early to catch the market for that subject.)

Dick also went to visit communes, during the late 60s and the early 70s, which had popped up all over the southwest. His draw to these communes was much more ephemeral. Had he been a child of the 60s generation, perhaps he, as a "lost child," might have found a sense of community and belonging in these sprawling, mostly dirty, collectives of well-meaning young people who were looking for a way to reconstruct their lives to have a greater, community purpose. When asked, Dick's view was that they were "mixed up kids," but that "their hearts were in the right place."

But no matter where Dick had traveled, he always had the tether-line of the wife and children back home, in his little house that felt more confining as the years went by. Dick decidedly had been in a crisis of faith, or you could say it was more basic than that. He had been in a crisis of meaning, and when that thirst for meaning became so acute that he could no longer tolerate it, he reached out to the long arm of religion, and it took him in and was balm for his wounds. He at least had a way to define himself now, even if he did not yet have a "home" where he belonged, internally.

P'oesay Apyan:

I have seen many people suffer in their lives, because they do not understand why we have this life. Sometimes, we saw that, because they had forgotten, the white men became lost in this struggle for meaning, and created complicated explanations, and never learned to move in the mind of the night, but remained, like children, in the mind of the day. I will explain.

We are spirit, and we reside for a short time in this human form, and after we leave it, we take on other forms. As we grow in our human experience, we are able to reach more and more frequently to the other side, to see our ancestors, to see our guides and teachers, and communicate with them directly. As we approach our physical death, these spirit connections become as important as our earthly ones, and finally we step over.

None of this is a cause for fear, and yet some belief systems have been created to turn humans from their own souls, from their own spirit knowledge. As they are separated from the elders, the ancestors, those from the other side, they lose the deepest part of their inner guidance. Their souls become so quiet that the voice becomes only a whisper, and sometimes is even silenced completely. This is what the tribe would call the soul death, and we have seen it happen to some. It is a sad thing, and it makes us weep. We go to our own guides, and we ask them if they can wake this sleeping spirit, if they can breathe new life into the soul. Sometimes they can, and sometimes they cannot. It depends upon whether the soul has given permission for an intervention at an earlier time, before the drama of this existence began. But we pray, we ask anyway, because none of us can know about the contract of another soul.

There is one thing that I have learned by watching rivers. The water of a river will never pass over the same rock twice in its journey to the sea. This is to say that the past will never return. The water of life flows over our experiences and moves on. To try to return to the past is as unnatural as a river that flows upstream. And many pains of the white men seem to have come from living in the remembrance of the past. The fresh water of life is flowing over them in every minute, yet they remain mired in the quicksand of their past mistakes and disappointments.

Sometimes white people would come to me, especially in my later years, and I could see that they were looking for answers to questions they could not even form in their minds. This is because their souls had become silent. They had become disconnected from their earth Mother, they were not embraced by their tribe, and they were filled with fear. When the animal is being pursued, he has no thought but to run. He does not see the sky. He does not feel the breeze. He does not know peace in his soul. He knows only to run, until the danger has passed. These white people who came to me were running from their fears, and the source of those fears was not known to them. This made it all more terrifying, and they ran harder. When they saw me, they saw that I was not running, and for them, this appeared as wisdom. They did not realize that not running is just the state of my being. It means that I am standing at the door. But wisdom lies on the other side. My soul must listen, to hear the guidance of spirit. Spirit must speak, through the soul, and from this comes wisdom. They did not realize that first they had to find peace, to stop running. Without that, wisdom could not even plant its seed.

~~~ ∫∫ ~~~

CHAPTER FOUR: EVERYTHING'S BROKEN

≈≈≈≈≈≈≈≈≈≈≈≈≈≈≈≈≈≈≈≈≈≈≈≈≈≈

Wilma's Story

Now comes the very sad part. My eldest daughter was in college, and my boy has just finished his junior year in high school. He was very tall, and had been Center on his basketball team for two years running, leading them to a state championship, averaging 26 points a game. The whole family would turn out for his games. His academic performance was faltering, but he was well-liked and respected, and was a great basketball player. He had a real passion for the sport. My eldest had completed her first year, and had a great boyfriend, very sweet and quiet, and was studying psychology. My middle daughter had lots of friends, and was happy, and my youngest was not far behind her. And Dick was gone again.

This time was different than the other times, though. He left in the middle of summer, which meant that all the irrigating was still to be done through the dry summer months, or the crops would fail. He had been gone a couple of days in summer, once or twice, but not enough to make a difference. We relied on that crop income to pay our mortgage each year, so I donned the hip-high "gator" boots and went out in the field, studied the sluice gates and slogged through the mud, trying to figure out how to redirect water so that it spilled out over the whole field without killing the young plants. The "sets" had to be moved every few hours, so I sweated it out with getting up at 5 am, getting to work, managing the household, paying the bills, and getting out there at night again to turn off the water flow so I could sleep some hours and be up again the next morning. At first, I was game, for a month or so. But then Dick called one day and said he had established himself in Bar Harbor, Maine, had gotten himself a construction job there, and thought he would "stay a while." "Stay a while?" I screamed, over the phone. "What do you mean, 'a while'? How long is that? And I guess I am just supposed to buck up and take care of all your responsibilities while you are gone without complaint? What has happened to you? Are you crazy?"

Well, I guess that was probably not the ideal word to use, because he simply said, "I am sorry, Wilma. I will be in touch," and the conversation was ended. I hung up the phone, and slumped on the piano bench, where we kept the phone, and I started to cry. They were quiet little sobbing tears, like a little girl makes who does not want to be heard. I didn't know where to start first, what to think about. Did this mean he was not coming back at all? Did I want to keep this farm if my husband was no longer helping? My son was almost out of high school, and it would then be just me and my daughters. It didn't make sense to stay, but how could I leave this place? It had been my home for ten years, and that was the longest I had lived anywhere.

Just then, my middle daughter came over to me, and said, "Hey, mom, what's for dinner?" But as she approached me, she saw the tears, and sat down next to me and put her arm around me. She said, "Was that Dad?" with the prescience of youth, and I nodded, trying desperately to hold back the waterworks. "When is he coming back?" She asked. "I don't know," I replied. I wasn't up to telling her yet that he had taken a job 2200 miles away. I wasn't able to accept it in my own mind yet.

I just got up and made the kids some dinner, went out to do the last irrigation set of the day, and headed back in to go to bed. I felt really, really weary. There was a fabulous sunset of oranges, and reds, greens and blues, that covered the whole sky. Colorado life was full of those sunsets, and it was one of the things I loved best about our farm: You could see those sunsets with a completely unobstructed view. No telephone lines, no houses, just open field and open sky. I looked up and took a deep breath, remembered our optimism when we moved to this place, and I wondered, what went so wrong? How did we get from there to here?

This all continued for a several months more. Mike entered his senior year, and basketball season began, and still no Dick. The crops were harvested. I hired a neighbor to do it, and he took a percentage, so we made less than usual, but I did pretty well, actually, considering that I knew nothing about irrigation previously. I had some extra cash, and actually started catching up on the bills. Dick had always paid them before, and I saw that his "system" had been less than systematic. I created a family budget, and stuck with it, so I gained confidence with each month that passed.

Mike was somewhat of a star, and scouts were beginning to take notice of him. We were there for the games each week, now in a little row of three, minus Dick. I think Mike felt his absence more than he let on. He seemed to be getting into conflicts in school more than he had previously, and became more distant. I was pretty sure that he was taking drugs (after all, this was 1970) but I had no idea how to talk to him about it. He had his own car, one of the wrecks that Dick had collected and had gotten running, so Mike pretty much made his own schedule. I felt this sense of foreboding, but other than trips to the principal's office here and there, nothing really bad happened.

There was one thing. One of Mike's close friends was a couple of years older than him. Jim was a precocious kid, a thinker, and I am pretty sure was the source of many of Mike's drug experiences. The guy had also befriended my tall shy daughter when she was finishing high school, and I think she had had a little "thing" for him, actually, though it was probably private and never realized. That year Jim died. His motorcycle ran into the middle of a train, and he died instantly. The odd thing was that the radio announced the death of a motorcyclist, and Mike called Shannon and told her that Jim was dead, before they had even identified the body. I think the death shook both of them, and cast a sad pallor over the family for a while.

My youngest daughter was also quieter than usual. She spent most of her time in her room reading. My middle daughter seemed mostly impervious and cheerful, but I suspected that it was a coping mechanism more than anything else, as I seemed to become less and less competent and getting meals on the table and keeping the household in order. I was just tired. I would have loved to have been able to take a little break myself, but that was not to be, apparently. Dick only wrote letters now, every few weeks, and enclosed most of his paychecks, addressed to me. He had opened a bank account in Bar Harbor, and those letters were not a source of happiness for me, but usually made me cry. There was something so depressing about seeing a check printed out to "Richard E. Roark" without the usual "Wilma J. Roark" next to it, and his scrawling hand addressing the check to me. It was so cold, and I knew each time it arrived how really alone I was. His letters were newsy and impersonal. He had gone lobstering, and learned about that industry. He was camping in Arcadia National Park in a little trailer he had bought, and it was beautiful there. He saw the geese going over in their migration. I missed him. He was the only real boyfriend or male companion I had ever known, and the letters made me miss and resent him more.

During those days, I felt a bitterness steep into my system. I began to suspect sometimes that I hated Dick, and I would fantasize telling him to "GET OUT!" if and when he ever showed up again. I had always hated my mother's negativity, especially about men, and my older sister was also filled with resentment, and had contracted breast cancer some years before. Now I was headed down the same road. I looked in the mirror, and saw myself aging. I was 45 now, and where was my life? My kids were teenagers, and didn't need me like they had before. My husband had abandoned me, and I was living on a ramshackle farm in Colorado, with no friends and no one to support me. But at least I had my job. My boss, Dick Chaney, was a sympathetic man, and while I did not confide in him fully, he knew that Dick was "away," and did what he could to make my life easier.

Then the bomb dropped. Chaney decided to retire. They were looking for a replacement, but in the meantime, they wondered if I could take over the day to day operations? I would chair the Chamber meetings each month, and continue to organize the lunches and events, like I had always done. I was happy to help, and the transition was a smooth one. In fact, it was almost too smooth. Within a couple of months, everyone noticed that things were running very smoothly, and began to compliment me about it. The monthly meetings were more lively, and we seemed to accomplish more with me at the helm. I began to wonder if they might consider making me, a woman, the new manager. After all, I had been there for 9 years and knew the office operation like the back of my hand. It was possible!

This became my ray of sunshine in what had become otherwise a pretty dispirited life. I began to come home and recount to my young daughters all my exploits of the day. They would say, "Way to go, Mom!" and I would feel a sense of personal pride in my work that was new to me. Women back then got little recognition in the workplace, especially in the business world. I felt special.

And then they found a replacement. They told me to write the letter of invitation to him, without any explanation to me at all of why I had not been chosen. It was as if no one had ever really considered me a candidate at all. And two weeks later, Ernie Witucki appeared at the office, and began to "run things." It was obvious that he felt threatened by me, and began to make my life miserable. He was arrogant, unpersonable, and I could not imagine why they had chosen him. He was openly hostile to my suggestions about anything, whereas in the past, Chaney had given my creativity free reign, and had enjoyed my enthusiasm. I began to come home with long complaints about my miserable days at the office with Witucki, who I now referred to as the "little prick."

I wrote to Dick and asked him to come home. I felt like things were unraveling. Mike's school career was finishing, and his team was winning, and Dick was not there to see it. I was tired, all the time now. I would get home and spend hours in my room. The girls could fend for themselves, and I started to buy more TV dinners, so they could put something in when they got home. I literally had nothing in my life that I was enjoying, and work was pure torture.

One day, I went to work, and I suddenly felt this rush of energy. Everything was funny again, and I started taking out construction paper, and making little decorations for springtime, to put around the office. When Ernie asked what I was doing, I ignored him, after explaining that I was decorating. I also told him that he could go "shove it" and called him a "stuffed shirt" when he asked me to type a letter. I told him, "You know how to do everything. Do it yourself!" and kept on cutting. Within a few hours, a few of the chamber men came in to visit with me. I had known them for years, and greeted them with warmth and enthusiasm, and they smiled back at me, and then went into Ernie's office and shut the door. A few minutes later they came out, and Ernie said, "Wilma, why don't you take the rest of the day off?" and I responded, "Why don't you take the rest of the day off? I am busy. What are you doing?" and I kept on cutting.

Another short conference behind closed doors, and this time Jim Draper came out and took my arm and said, "Wilma, you need to go home now." I looked up at him, and tears welled up in my eyes, and I realized what was happening. I was being fired. I felt shocked. After all I had done. I had poured myself into that little office with body and soul. I had made that little office what it was. And now this new guy, who didn't know how to do anything, had come in and had displaced me in a few short months. Because I was a woman, and I didn't matter. Just like that, it was over.

I got in the car, and drove home, and encountered my littlest daughter, who had come home on the bus. My middle daughter was with the track team at her school that day. She asked me, surprised, "Mom, you're home early!" I told her, "Yes, that's right! Let's celebrate!" and started pulling out ingredients to make a cake. But somehow, I then decided to pull out all the ingredients in the cabinets, let them breathe a little, and then I decided to give the dogs peanut butter, and then I wanted to give all the pets some people food. My little one was watching me, wide-eyed, for a while, and then she quietly disappeared.

A couple hours later she arrived with my middle daughter, who had caught a ride home early from track. I guess Erin had ridden her bike to the school to get her. They both looked at me, and at each other, and went in the other room to talk. It was like what had happened at the office, so I got mad at them, and started to yell at them both. Then I started to cry, and they comforted me for a while and I went to bed.

I don't remember how it all happened, from that point on, but I know my son was on hand, and then a policeman came a few days later, and politely offered me a ride in his car. The kids were there, and encouraged me to take it. I didn't want to, and then the policeman grabbed me and put handcuffs on me, and said that I had to go. My middle daughter was crying, and my son said, "Don't worry Mom, we will be right behind you in my car." And just like that, I became a hospital patient at the regional hospital.

The next time I saw Dick, it was "from behind bars." So began what was easily the most painful period of my life. Childhood had been hard, adolescence confusing, marriage disappointing, but this was just painful. Hopeless, helpless and painful.

~~~ ∬ ~~~

So what was taking place with Wilma's soul during this period of her life? She had experienced a sense of partnership with Dick when they bought and fixed up the farm. She had discovered a sense of accomplishment and pride in raising her children and working at a job she enjoyed and did well. She had begun to feel settled, and had just begun to explore the idea of a deeper meaning in life.

Her husband on the other hand was well into his exploration of deeper meaning. He had begun to write a book of his spiritual insights, which he kept locked in a metal box under his bed. He believed that God had spoken to him with cloud formations one day, and told him that he was meant to go to Russia to help convert that Godless nation to Christianity. While Wilma was finally becoming grounded in reality and stabilized, Dick was secretly and quietly going off the deep end.

One day, listening to his inner "guidance," Dick purchased a one-way to ticket to Moscow. The flight flew out of Boston, and was departing in one week's time. He had just enough time to get there, if he left immediately. He packed up while the house was empty, and in a euphoria of religious fervor, he set out of for Boston. He knew that God would provide for his family while he was on this important mission. The hardest part was saying goodbye to his dog, who had become his constant companion in recent years. But one does not hesitate when the Lord calls, so he was off.

He arrived at Boston with great enthusiasm, with plenty of time for the flight. He parked his van in a space where it could stay a few months, and took a taxi to the airport. When his flight was called, he went to the counter with confidence. This is when his confidence was shaken. The ticket agent was doggedly insistent on a point he had not considered. He had obtained a passport, but he did not have return ticket. He was planning to stay for as long as God called him to stay. He explained this to the agent, but she was unmoving. Dick was grounded. He had not brought money with him. He believed that God had directed him that he would live as Christ had, on the kindness of others. He had only $30 in his wallet, and had left his checkbooks at the farm.

After slumping in the airport for a few hours, he had an idea. He would go up to Maine, and get a job, and earn the money for the return flight. The plan was not called off, but simply delayed. He took another taxi to his van, and headed north.

When he first called Wilma, it was two weeks later, and he had received his first paycheck. He could feel that she was shocked at the news that he had taken a job in Maine. "Are you leaving me?" she asked softly. It had not occurred to him that she might come to that conclusion. He needed to demonstrate to her that this was not his intention, but if he told her of the Russia plan--- well, that just couldn't happen. He could not have someone ridicule his dream. So he told her that he had just received a paycheck, and would be sending it to her, and would continue to do that every two weeks, so she would not have to worry. He didn't add, "until I come back," because after all, who knew what God had in store for him.

So then Dick sat down at the picnic table in his campground and did his own calculations. He knew what it cost to run the farm and the household, because he had done it for years. He knew how much Wilma made, and the amount of his disability check. When he added it all up, he realized that she didn't have much of a margin to work with, and without some assistance from him, she might not be able to make ends meet. He was also aware that he was leaving her with the irrigating, and wasn't that sure she would be able to do it. If the crops failed, they could lose the farm.

Dick got down on his knees and prayed about what to do. Then he divided up his paycheck into three parts. The biggest part was for Loveland, the smallest part was to support him in Maine, and the other part was to save for his ticket back from Russia.

The plan was not scrapped, but just delayed. It would take a few months to earn the money for Russia at this rate. But he knew he could do it. God had brought him this far.

On a soul level, Dick had already reached his breaking point. It was not enough to be a Christian and do nothing. He needed to find a way to serve his Savior. He instinctively knew that his life as a recluse on his farm served no one. In his soul's desperate need to find meaning for his life, he literally reached for the skies, and found the first shred of meaning that appeared to him.

Dick was a practical man, and had not cultivated his imagination much in his life. He knew the practicalities of life, and the only "miracles" that he was aware of had taken place in the Bible. He was not someone to note coincidences, or experience moments of blind inspiration. Yet his soul needed to breathe. He needed a way for God to speak to him more directly. He needed a "sign." The deep longing in his soul made him look up one day and see the "sign" he had been seeking in two cloud formations, one in the shape of a hammer and sickle, the symbol of Russia, and the other in the shape of cross. He had been reading about Russian missionaries, and this had captured his imagination. He wanted to believe so badly that he created a reality. This was his soul's attempt to touch greatness.

Dick at this point in his life was no longer a father and husband. He was a child crying desperately to find his own father, the father he had never had as a child, who would love and direct him. You might say that he had regressed, and in his hunger to make that connection, all the rest of his life faded and even disappeared. This was Dick's soul's journey at this stage of his life. He had finally come face to face with the gaping hole in his own upbringing.... the absence of the nurturing, care, and affection that is usual for children in healthy homes.

You might say that Wilma was just at the wrong place at the wrong time. In her life, she had begun to spread her wings, feel confident, and heal her old wounds. And she was ready to explore a deeper meaning for life. Dick's unexpected departure sent her back in a downward spiral, in which she again saw herself as insignificant, and her needs as unimportant to others, especially to her husband. She was alone again, unloved again, and it was up to her to be independent again. Her focus returned again to survival, for herself and her children. At least she understood her role well as a mother, and she would not let her babies go hungry. She would do what was required of her. In that sense, her decisions were easy. She would knuckle down and take care of things. But in her heart, a deep wound had reopened. It was her wound of childhood, of her feelings being disregarded, of her needs being ignored. She felt quietly invisible.

The one place of relief, where she could still feel important and appreciated, was at her job. When that final piece disintegrated before her, her emotional world and her mental world could no longer keep things together. She approached a dangerous split within herself, a separation took place, and her conscious mind stopped working within the grounding of physical reality. As they say, she was "in her own world," and there would be no returning to the past now.

~~~ ∫∫ ~~~

And what was taking place on the level of spirit for Wilma? She was discovering another aspect of her soul's contract with Dick. He was not there only to appreciate her (which he had done), and encourage her creativity. He also had been chosen by her soul to abandon her, to once again put her soul to that test, so that she could once and for all face those false securities that come from other's opinions, and learn to value herself as herself and for herself. Had Dick remained a faithful and supportive husband, Wilma would not have reached as deeply inside to discover and confront her dragons. She had chosen a very hard path in life, remember, from childhood on. And Dick was the perfect candidate to ultimately provide that final disappointment that would cause the crack in the armor of false confidence, and put her face to face with herself.

And Wilma, with her helplessness, would be the one person that could draw Dick back from the web of illusion that he had created for himself. He was fond of her, though he perhaps at this stage he still lacked the capacity for true love. But he valued loyalty, and she was very loyal. He could not fully abandon her, so while he was now the cause of Wilma's social demise, she was the source of his salvation. She saved her husband from a life of selfishness and delusion, by calling him back to reality and responsibility. Their two paths became even more deeply entwined by this latest turn of events.

Of course, when Wilma was committed to the mental hospital, Mike, Kelley and Erin immediately wrote to their father to tell him. They also discovered the phone number for the campground where he was staying, and managed to get a message to him. One phone call later, and he was back on the road, returning to the farm. He knew that hospital bills were expensive, even with insurance coverage. His Mission to Russia would just have to wait. Dick returned to Colorado.

P'oesay Apyan:

In our family, suffering was understood as part of life. It came in many forms over our lives-- sometimes through sickness, sometimes through the unkindness of others. Sometimes earth Mother herself dealt us a blow, with a tornado or a big storm. My family was my tribe, and it was strong because we were many, and because we moved together as one.

Sometimes I would feel confusion when hardship fell upon me. When my mother was very sick, and I realized from her eyes that she would be leaving me, I was just a little boy. I remembered sitting on my mother's lap, feeling all cradled with her strength, feeling her behind my back and her arms all around me. Her coat would surround us and keep out the cold. I could sit there and look out as if I were a young bear in a warm cave, and the world looked so beautiful and complete in those moments.

Now she was lying flat, and had become very thin. They told me it was the illness of my mother's mothers, and her spirit would be leaving to join our ancestors soon. I felt a feeling I had never felt before inside. It felt like there was an animal in there who was starting to wail. It was angry and wanted to hit something, but it was also so filled with emptiness, it was almost hollow, and all of the sudden tears were flowing out, so I ran out to the tree mothers and sat with them, and let the water from my eyes fill the earth.

I sat until the sobbing stopped, and the tears stopped flowing. It was late afternoon, and the sunlight was coming through the high branches of the trees, reaching down to the earth in patterns of light and dark, and as I sat, I began to see the insects moving in the soil, and buzzing around the flowering plants. I could hear their wings moving all around me, and I realized that I was surrounded by the life of Mother. I felt myself relax back into the trunk of the tree that supported me, and I looked up at the blue of the sky, between the trees. It was calm and cool. I turned and smelled the strong smell of the bark behind me, and felt it scraping against my cheek and I put one arm around my tree mother and let myself relax and sleep. Then I went back to the village.

My birth mother died the following day. We prepared a beautiful goodbye for her. We carried her on a flat bed into the forest, and found a clearing with a blending light and shadow in a dance of yellows, greens, and browns. We put her tenderly on the ground, and covered her with fragrant dry leaves. We knew that she was resting comfortably for her return to mother Earth. Then we formed a circle around her, and we held our hands and made the circle complete, and we turned ourselves up to the sky mother, and we all wailed together, a song of sadness and strength. We said goodbye to my mother, and we freed her soul to return to our ancestors. I looked around me and I saw that all our eyes were wet. We allowed our grief to leave our souls and released it to the skies, and it flew away on the breeze.

Then we released our hands and returned to the village, and had our dinner. The men had caught a fresh deer that day, and the venison meat tasted particularly strong and good that night. The fire's light somehow seemed brighter, and as I looked around at the faces of my family around me, I felt filled with love and appreciation that they were still my "cave," and that earth Mother still surrounded me, fed me, and cared for me. I slept deeply that night, and woke up the next day to a new life without my birth mother.

In my tribe, we have always understood that life contains disappointments. When one of us struggles against the events of Fate, the elders remind us that we are guests of our earth Mother, and that all that we receive from her is a gift, whether it is something easy or something difficult. Our elders remind us that all of life's experiences cause us to grow deeper in our connection to earth and expand our knowledge of Spirit.

Our elders remind us that in nature, nothing is wasted. When an animal dies, its flesh feeds the family of another. The leaves fall from the trees and become the soil that our food grows in. The lightning strikes and burns the forest, and the animals run for shelter from the blazes. But after the fire, nature is fed the rich ash of the tree mothers who have sacrificed to feed the soil again, and enrich it to continue to feed us for generations to come. Storms come and flood the valleys, and when the water recedes, it leaves mudflats that are filled with frogs that the birds come and eat, making them become strong and grow in number. Nothing is wasted.

When I was an old man, I saw many white men whose faces showed suffering and disappointment. They did not understand that everything that comes to us is a gift to help us grow and make us strong. They saw the darkness, but did not see that it was intertwined with light, like the forest floor the day that my mother was returned to the Earth. Because of this, they often felt unloved and uncared for. They had become blind to the fact that the earth Mother is feeding them the air that they breathe, in every second of the day, and that the soils never cease from producing foods for them to eat, that the trees stand to give them shelter, and that the rivers give them fish and living water. They feel abandoned and alone, when Mother herself is cradling them, even as they look downward and inward with their sad eyes. This was the blindness that we saw so often in the white men, the blindness we prayed for a cure for, when we saw it in each other. Their spirits were asleep, and we prayed for their awakening, so that they could love and appreciate the many gifts of family, of life. So that they could live in joy over the miracle of existence!

~~~ ∫∫ ~~~

CHAPTER FIVE:
COMPLICATED TIMES

≈≈≈≈≈≈≈≈≈≈≈≈≈≈≈≈≈≈≈≈≈≈≈≈

Wilma's Story

It is so hard for me to tell you this part of my story. To merely say that it was sad would be to ignore so many moments in which I felt complete despair about every aspect of my life. Can you imagine what it felt like, the first time they took my clothes off, while I fought them tooth and nail, and put me first in a shapeless blue hospital garb, with no underwear and a gaping back, and then fitted me into a "straightjacket"? I didn't even think those things were legal, but there I was, being shuffled down the hallway with my arms pinned across my chest, screaming bloody murder, because they couldn't exactly muzzle me, cursing them in every way I could, even spitting when I had a chance.

I felt so helpless, and panicked. Somewhere in the back of my mind, I registered the eyes of the other patients I passed in the hall, as several strong orderlies escorted me to my room. They were flat, unemotional. I realized that they had seen this scene before. When I got to my room, they laid me on a small hard bed, put a needle in my arm (there was a hole in the jacket for that purpose), and then left the room without even looking back or saying goodbye. It was like they had deposited a package.

This wasn't a package! This was my life! And I had just lost everything! I started to cry, and cry, and cry. I think that wailing would be the right word for it. I felt so much pain inside of me, and confusion, that I didn't even know where to put it. I wanted to reach out to someone or something to help me, but I knew there wasn't anyone. No one could help me here. I have no idea how long I cried, but then a new nightmare began. I began to feel this sleepiness, but it was so strong. My muscles felt funny, all constricted in this hard fabric, and stiff, from the inside out. I know that my mind was confused at that time, that my judgment was impaired, but I thought I was dying. I figured that they had poisoned me with that needle, and were leaving me to die. I felt a new wail of sadness overwhelm me as I realized that I would never see my darling children again. They started to parade in front of me, coming back to me at all their different ages, the towheaded babies, the independent teens, the young adults, holding puppies up to me, showing me their schoolwork. I missed them. I started calling, "Kids, kids!"

"Shannon, Mike! Kelley! Erin! Come here quick! I am dying! They are killing me!" I had to say goodbye. I had to see them one more time before this darkness overtook me.

But they didn't come, and I finally slept. And that was how my first experience of the mental hospital happened. When I woke up, I was in the same room, and there were no windows, so I had no idea what time it was. My mouth was impossibly dry, and felt numb like I had taken Novocain. There was a nurse there, with her back to me. I realized that I had wetted myself in my sleep. She was unwinding me and telling me, "So will you behave, Wilma, so we can leave these things off of you?" I tried to mimic her, saying with a snotty voice, "Will you behave, Wilma, so we can leave these things off of you?" But it came out as unintelligible drivel. She seemed to get what I was doing though, because I saw her half-smile. She gestured to some water, and said, "you will need that," and asked me to take some pills. She told me if I didn't, they would have to inject me again. I took the pills, looking at her warily, and put them in my mouth. She left, and I spit them out. She came back in, found them on the floor, and gave me some new ones. This time she watched as I took them.

I realized that if I were going to escape from this place, it was going to take some ingenuity.

They let me go out into a central room, where a lot of other heavily drugged patients were sitting around in ill-fitting, baggy, and indiscrete clothing. No one seemed to care much about anything really. The food was bland, the therapies were boring, and the days were interminable. My family came to see my every day, but visiting hours were very short. I didn't really understand why I was there. I was fine now. I didn't think that I had done anything that off the wall in the first place, but now I was on my "best behavior," except that I couldn't help but mimic and ridicule the orderlies whenever I got the chance. I was no harm to anyone, but they kept me there two weeks. And when they let me out, it was on the condition that I would take these little pills every day for the rest of my life. Like THAT was going to happen. But even my family was insistent, so I said I would, to appease them.

Of one thing I was sure: I was NEVER going back into a mental hospital again.

Oh, and another change, besides my losing my job, losing my dignity, being stuck with needles, and incarcerated in a mental hospital--- Dick was back.

He first appeared at the hospital, with the others, but didn't really attempt to speak to me alone. I figured that the setting was not conducive to the long apology and explanation that he owed me for his ten month absence. He just gave me a perfunctory hug, and sort of organized the kids in the "coming and going" part of the visits. I avoided looking at him, and refused to speak with him. The kids were talkative enough that it was hardly noticeable until we got into the car and were riding home. That time, it was just him and me, since the kids were at school.

He asked me, "So how are you today? Feeling better?" when we got in the car, after my suitcase/overnight bag was situated. "Feeling better?" I retorted, almost stupefied. "Yes, I feel GREAT now!" I responded, with all the sarcasm I could muster. He didn't attempt any more conversation on the way home. I stole a glance at him out of the corner of my eye, and saw that his mouth was set in that hard straight line that I knew he got when we was really upset, and trying to maintain control, and his eyes were narrowly focused on the road. I knew that it probably hurt, knowing what he had done to me. But, hell! Was that really the best he could do? "How are you today?" Where was, "Oh Wilma, I am so sorry. I am sorry that I abandoned you and your life fell apart before your eyes, and now you have humiliated yourself before the only community you have ever really wanted to call home, have no job, and are stuck with a husband who doesn't give a shit." No, just "How are you today." This was the husband I was married to. This was my Knight in Shining Armor who would rescue me from the dragons.

To say that I felt bitterness now would be understatement. I hated him with everyone in me who had ever hated anyone for making fun of me, for ignoring me, for yelling at me, for abandoning me....... it was like all those "me's" had somehow come together inside me with a big ball of rage and resentment, and then directed it all at Dick. He was the personification of everything that had ever gone wrong in my life. And now I was stuck with him. When we pulled up at the farm, and the engine was turned off, I broke the silence with, "I want a divorce." He didn't reply. But now at least he knew, unequivocally, that I blamed him for all of this.

The dogs rushed up to see me, and I felt their licks and wet noses with such intense pleasure. I looked up. It was summer, and the trees were full of leaves in our little oasis in the countryside. I saw the red barn with its white trim and Pennsylvania Dutch good luck sign I had painted. The horses had come into the whitewashed corral, as if they had known and wanted to be there for my homecoming. I went out and hugged Diablo's big strong neck for a while, and felt the tension start to fall away. Then I went inside, to my own bed, and slept.

~~~ ʃʃ ~~~

This was what anyone would call a "dark night of the soul" for Wilma. She had known some difficult times in her life. She had felt loneliness and abandonment. But she had never touched upon the kind of pain that she experienced at becoming hospitalized. The shock of the experience made it very difficult to really process what had taken place. At this point, you might say that she was in "denial." She knew that things had gotten a little "out of hand" at the office, but lots of people resigned their jobs in anger, and she hadn't been that rude. The police escort to the hospital was a little more confusing. She knew her kids must have called the police, but why? She had no doubt that they were on her side. What had she done, to make them think she was unsafe? In her mind, there was continual cognizance through the whole experience. She had always known she was Wilma. It was life that was incomprehensible and out of control, not her. She alternately tried to make sense of it, and tried not to think about it. She was just certain that this experience could NEVER happen again. It was behind her, and now she had to put her life back together.

She attempted to talk to her middle daughter about the experience, to ask her why they had called the police. She just replied, "Mom, you were acting really, really strange, saying things that didn't make sense, and we didn't know what to do. We called Dr. Anderson to ask his advice, and he said he didn't know, we should ask the police. They told us that it sounded like you were having a "nervous breakdown," and probably needed to go get evaluated and get some medications. Since you refused to go, they said they needed to take you, for your own good......"

But then she burst into tears, and said, "But Mom, we never knew it would be like that! That place was horrible. If we had known, we would have never taken you there!" Wilma hugged her and comforted her as best she could, while she attempted to digest what she had just heard. Was it possible that she could no longer trust her own perception of things? Was she "mentally ill"? What would that mean for her from now on?

What happens to the soul of a person when the bottom falls out of her life? Wilma had always had a somewhat fragile ego. She had been ridiculed as a child, and berated by an angry and largely unsympathetic mother. She had endured the gradual withdrawal of her husband, and had no social life to speak of, save her children and her job. Now she had to digest the complete disintegration of whatever semblance of order she had been able to produce in her life after her husband had abandoned her. What was next?

What had really happened to Wilma on a soul level was that she had discovered that she was truly alone. While it appeared that she was surrounded by the shelter of family and home, all of that could be gone in an instant, leaving her completely alone, and helpless. This shook her confidence, and her fragile ego, to the core.

And she could no longer trust. She could not trust institutions such as work, nor hospitals, as a place of assistance and healing. Nor trust her husband and life partner, as a source of support and understanding. Nor, and most importantly, trust herself, her own mind, as an accurate interpreter of reality. Wilma was reeling, and it would be a long time before she would be able to get her feet back on the ground.

At first, she rested, and reveled in the comforts of home. Dick went out and immediately got a job, so she knew he would be staying for a while. After all, she had just lost her salary. Very quickly, she realized that they would need the extra income. She still had two daughters in school, moving toward graduation. So after a couple of months, Wilma went out looking. Chaney gave her a glowing recommendation, and she got a job with R.S.V.P., the Retired Seniors Volunteer Program, as a receptionist and secretary. She really liked this job, because she acted as a kind of hostess for various programs, and was really quite good with the old people. She got to do her little decorations and art work again for different events, and things went quite well for nearly a year. Her eldest daughter entered her junior year of high school, her youngest finishing junior high, her son was in college. Dick was still there, and working. At first, she had dutifully taken the pills, but after a while, they were shoved in a corner of the medicine cabinet, and were gathering dust.

Both her daughters had "gotten religion" in the last year or so, and she ferried them to bible studies in the evening, and watched them tote their bibles to school every day. She was curious, and asked them about their experiences. They told her that they felt love from God, and that they had confessed their sins and were now saved and "baptized in the Spirit."

All of this sounded good to Wilma, and she began to attend charismatic meetings at the Episcopal Church, where the family had attended Christmas and Easter services for years. She enjoyed the camaraderie of the meetings, and dutifully said the prayers, sang the songs, and even "spoke in tongues" along with others. But one day she confessed to her daughters that she was not sure that she was really "feeling" it. It seemed somewhat artificial to her. She wasn't really sure that God would want to send everyone to hell, unless they confessed their sins. It just didn't make sense to her, though she loved the music and the message of hope. Wilma privately thought there must be something wrong with her, because the rest of them seemed to be so taken by the experience, and she could not really "get it."

Then, one day, Wilma was very surprised to come home, open the newspaper, and discover that Jesus was coming soon, it was the Millennium, and all this information had been written in code, in a way that apparently only SHE could understand. When the kids got home from school, she went to them with great excitement, and showed them the newspaper, and told them the great news. They didn't seem to get it, and told her, "No, Mom. That is just a regular newspaper," and she realized that, if they could not see it, and only SHE could see it, then she must be truly special. She was some sort of oracle, or perhaps a saint, here to help others toward Heaven. And then it hit her like a flash: She herself was the Messiah! She ran to her kids with this new revelation, completely beside herself with joy at all the good things that were to come. They didn't receive the news as positively as she would have hoped, but no matter. They would come to understand.

Then Dick came home from work, and she turned away from him, and started arranging some furniture in a way that would block the door. She felt some foreboding, some sinister presence. He touched her arm briefly to restrain her, and she was struck with another thunderbolt of understanding. DICK was the devil! And she was here to save the world from him! She ran to the kitchen for a knife, anything she could find to scare him away from her family, to fulfill her role as Savior. In the scuffle that ensued, she heard her husband say over his shoulder to their daughters, "Girls! Call the police!"

Somewhere in the back of Wilma's overcharged brain, she realized. It was happening again. This time, by the time the police came, she was willing to go peacefully. When she got to the hospital, they recognized her and said hello. She got into her hospital robe voluntarily, and took the heavy medication that made her drowsy orally instead of by injection. When they had tried to inject her, this was the only time that she had shouted, "NO!" in terror, and an understanding orderly gave her the option of taking the pills through her mouth. She was locked in her room, but at least there was no straightjacket, and this time, her family had packed her a little bag, which looked at her comfortingly from the corner of the room, as she felt that horrible freezing sensation come over her muscles and knew that she was sinking into another dreamless sleep.

~~~ ʃʃ ~~~

Now what can be said for what happens to a person's spirit, when it succumbs to mental illness? What caused Wilma's life to take this disastrous turn? Of course, there is the argument of genetics. She had a nephew who was bipolar, and while at this point she was being diagnosed as schizophrenic, mental illness was known to run in families. She had also had a fairly serious car accident six months before the onset of the illness, and late onset manic depression had been connected with head injuries, in the scientific research. So for Wilma, was this just the luck of the draw? A predisposition, combined with negative experiences which triggered the illness? Or was there something else at work here?

To understand and even to accept how mental illness can have a place in the evolution of the soul, a person has to look at the nature of experience itself. We feel things through the sensors of our bodies, and through the filter of our emotions. The emotions have varying degrees of intensity. You might consider that the more blinding and whiter the heat to which a metal is subjected, the more quickly it can soften and be molded into something more beautiful. While on the surface, Wilma's soul decision to descend into the realm of mental illness might seem incomprehensible, consider the whiteness of the light to which she would now be subjected. Her tragedies would no longer be at the level of a child's disappointing school performance, or the loss of a job, or an errant husband. Now her dramas would play themselves out in truly epic proportions. Hers would no longer be a paltry, average existence. Her tragedy would now be dramatic, powerful, and the experiences that were to follow in the rest of her earthly life would constantly push her to the edge of her ability to tolerate, assimilate, suffer, and understand. She would be forced to learn to communicate, love, and survive under the harshest of conditions. Her soul would truly be "put to the test." Wilma was now moving out of a sleepy understanding of life to a double dose of the worst, and the best, that existence can offer.

Her spirit was ready for this. Wilma was a person of extraordinary compassion. Hers was a truly giving spirit, and a frustration in her life was not having a sufficient vehicle to give more. She was also a person whose childhood injuries and pains were buried very, very deeply. She had succeeded in growing thick scar tissue over the wounds of her childhood during those first years in Colorado, but the wounds remained, and had begun to fester. This illness, and these hospitalizations, would tear the thickened cover off those wounds, and they would begin to see the light of day, and experience the fresh water of awareness. Hers would not be an easy road, and it would be a long road, before this journey ended with her frozen in another hospital bed, years from now. But these years would not be wasted. Wilma did not realize it, but her spirit had just graduated.

P'oesay Apyan:

I would like to explain that the mind has two homes. There is the home of the day, the home that takes care of family, that hunts, that experiences the forest and feels the sun. This home of the mind is the one a child is born into, and lives within for all of life, until the spirit leaves the body.

The other home of the mind is the home of the night, or the spirit home. This home is not as easy to find for the mind and soul of a person. It is hidden in darkness at birth, but as the child grows into a man, this other spirit home becomes stronger, and the mind spends more and more delightful hours in this home of the night, in which other spirits also dwell, and can communicate with one's spirit mind.

When a person's mind resides only in the home of the day, and never graduates to the home of the night, this person is considered by the tribe to be "simple." This is to say that the person retains the mind of the child, and the deeper workings of spirit will not be known for this person. These child-persons are revered among my people as pure souls; they are cherished and treated as royalty until they pass back into the spirit realm.

But there is another story that sometimes takes place in the mind of a person. Sometimes, the mind becomes lost between the two homes, the home of the day and the home of the night. When this occurs, the person must wander in silence until he can find his way to either the home of the day, or the home of the night. He is silent, because unless he remains in the home of the day, he cannot communicate with his family and tribe. And unless he is in the home of the night, he cannot communicate with his spirit guides and the elders in the spirit realm. So when a person's mind becomes lost between the homes of the night and the day, he is completely and totally alone.

For us, to be lost between the mind's two homes is the cruelest of tortures. This is because we understand that all of life is One, is a Unity, and we are one with all our brothers and sisters, both in the earthly day and in the spirit night. So when we lose our mind's way, we have lost our foundation, and we no longer know who we are. We have become invisible to ourselves, and this is the deepest of sufferings.

I have seen few individuals lost between these two homes, within our tribe. I have seen many more among the white man's culture. We believe that this is due to their use of "spirits," which is what they sometimes call alcohol. When the tribesmen tried alcohol, they discovered that the mind could not remain in the home of day, and that when they attempted to communicate with spirits in the home of the night, the spirits had fallen silent. This made many of us suspect that the white man's "spirits" of alcohol were a poison to the mind, and would eventually cause it to wander lost between its two homes.

We did see that sometimes for a time in their lives, members of the tribe would have a period in which the mind wandered alone, between the two homes. This would be after a deep tragedy, such as the loss of a child. Often, a mother's grief would be so deep, that she would no longer be able to communicate in the realm of the day, and her mind would be attempting to communicate with night spirits while not fully in the home of the day or night, and what would result was confusion. Neither her earthly family nor her spirit family could understand her while she wandered between homes. Also, and more rarely, it might happen when a warrior experienced extreme pain, as from a wound. These departures from the mind's homes would be briefer, and the warrior would often find his way back to the home of the day very quickly, and would return to us, or else he would decide to go into the home of the night, and his spirit might go to join his elders forever.

One thing we were able to see, with those whose minds were lost between the night and day. They were alone, and no one in the heavens or on the earth could reach in and pull them out of their confusion. This was a journey that they must take alone. When they re-emerged, once again to move easily between the home of the day and home of the night, and to communicate in each of them, we observed a deeper wisdom had resulted from their suffering. It was our belief that this wander was a supreme test, which we called the "Test of the Silver Way," because all suffering and experience on the earth has a reward in the deepening of the spirit's wisdom, just as great heat helps to realize the beauty of silver.

And in the way of my people, there is no reward greater than wisdom.

~~~ ∫∫ ~~~

CHAPTER SIX:
ANOTHER BEGINNING

≈ ≈

Wilma's story:

My second hospitalization was very different from the first. This time, after the anti-psychotic medicine had taken effect, I realized that I was not Jesus Christ after all. I realized that I was a very confused woman, with a brain that was no longer normal. I was no longer able to handle life.

This was a very sobering realization. In a way, the denial of the last year and a half was a picnic compared to how I felt now. I guess you could say that I felt flat. I now understood the flat, expressionless gazes that were turned on me during my first, dramatic entrance to Poudre Valley Hospital. This being "crazy" was a complete game-changer. Unless I could figure this out...... well, right now, to be honest, I had no clear image of my own future. All I could see was a blank. Everything else was still there--- the kids, the farm, my husband. The part that didn't seem to fit in anymore was me. Who was I now?

This visit was different for other reasons, also. This time I started paying more attention the drugs they were giving me. There was something called Haldol that the doctors seemed to love, and I hated. It made my mouth like cotton, made me completely constipated, and made my mouth so unresponsive to my thoughts that all I could do was mumble. Oh, and it also made me drool.

I won't say that I am a particularly vain woman. But I always liked to look "put together." I had several colors of lipstick that I used regularly, and since I had a kind of olive skin tone, deep reds looked somewhat natural on me, with my wavy dark hair. And I liked wearing clothes with a little color, mostly in earth tones. What I didn't like was wearing misshapen sweat pants and slippers, with some shirt that Dick had dug out of my drawers, because of course he had never noticed what I wore and didn't wear. But here in the hospital, there was no way to look good. My hair became frizzy because of the all the meds and the hospital diet. My eyes were glazed and unnatural-looking when I looked at myself in the mirror. And my mouth had that slack and discontented line to it. I guess that looking into the mirror and seeing myself put together had been one of the small pleasures of life for me. In short, now looking into a mirror was a horror---nothing but a reminder of this stranger that

I had become. I was gaining water weight, was constipated, and physically uncomfortable most of the time. My hands and feet twitched and it was hard to sit still, so I found myself wandering aimlessly in the halls of the hospital like an old woman. The mirror should have grounded me again, and instead it made me feel more alienated. Especially my eyes.

This visit was different too because I recognized a couple of the other patients this time around, and I realized that I was not the only one who was cycling in and out of hospitals with mental illness. Apparently, this world that now imprisoned me was reality for lots of other people, too. It was all kinds of sad to consider that, to wonder about all of their lives and their families, and how many people they were disappointing too, just like I was---in here instead of visiting my son at college, or talking to my daughter in Oregon on the phone about the upcoming birth of her first child. I tried to imagine the lives the others around me were leaving behind, what they had done for a living, how many dreams had been shattered by a hospital straightjacket, as mine had. These other patients were not just furniture to me this time around. They were real people. There were broken lives behind those eyes.... the laughter and optimism of youth and the promise of adulthood, consumed by the devouring appetite of mental illness. And I was one of them now. I felt an odd kinship, knowing that they suffered quietly as much as I did, and it gave me a small comfort.

No, life was not easy, was it Sarah? Or Burt, or Mary.... There were teenagers there, too. Other than their ages, they were indistinguishable from the rest of us. Their eyes held the same flatness hiding the same pathos.

And there was another huge change this time. It turned out that the regional hospital, Poudre Valley, could only take mental patients for short term care. So when I was not better after two weeks, they had to find someplace to ship me off to. Problem was that the next nearest facility was in Denver, 60 miles away from Loveland. I had to go in a hospital van, but my family followed me there, to get me settled in. I had to give Dick one thing; he was there like clockwork, any time something was needed at the hospital. I could give him a list of things to bring from the farm, and he would do his best to find them and bring them, usually enlisting the girls to help him. It was heartbreaking to see how they tried to come up with things to cheer me up at the hospital. They knew how I loved our dogs and cat, so they brought me their stuffed animals, or bought me one at the hospital store. They tried to combat the sterility of the hospital environment by bringing useless, silly little knickknacks from home. They made jokes about my situation, about my baggy pants. I could see by the way they treated me, all of them, that they still believed in me. I hoped they would not get worn out by this process, because those gifts meant more to me than they could know.

So when I had to go 60 miles away, instead of 15, that also meant that the almost daily visits would stop. I was on my own again. It was not as severe as the first hospitalization, when my mind had created a kind of painful isolation that I hoped to never experience again. But still, it was damn lonely, being driven so far away from all of them. And when you are hospitalized for mental illness, it is not like they will let you slip out for a couple of hours to say goodbye to the old homestead. And I was also to find out that when you are mentally ill, nobody knows how long it will last---when you will be able to go home again.

So I guess you could say that the drive to Ft. Logan Mental Hospital taught me something about patience. I could rage against all the injustice that was my life. But what good would it do? So I was just one more docile "Looney tune" in the van that day, staring ahead and trying not to focus on all the sad thoughts that crowded into my head. At least my family would be there when I arrived. That was more than many of the others with me would have today. Once again, I hoped to hell that my family would never stop believing in me.

And when they were there when I arrived, smiling and toting some goofy bunny to christen my new room, I cried with gratitude. And I have to admit, Ft. Logan was a little nicer. It was also way scarier, because here they had the permanent crazies, and you could hear them sometimes, wailing at night or in scuffles with orderlies in the hallway when we were supposed to be resting. But the food was better here, and they let us eat in the cafeteria with our families if we were not too bad off. We could wear street clothes, and my closet had space for some of my things. My room was bigger, and I didn't have to share with anyone. I can't say it was like a hotel room, but they did let me personalize it a bit. Some people had been there awhile, and it almost seemed like their rooms were "home" for them. This was both encouraging and discouraging to me at the same time. The therapies started to make more sense, also. They talked about coping with the disappointments, patients talked about the challenges of looking for work when you have a history of mental illness.

Young girls who had been suicidal talked about what had brought them to this point.

I know this will sound weird, but by the end of my stay at Ft. Logan, I had started reaching out to the patients around me. I could see that I was more clear-headed than most of them, and I would give them words of encouragement. I also had my sense of humor to fall back on, and it gave me no end of pleasure to make these "sourpusses" laugh at my jokes. If I had to make those jokes at the expense of me or someone else, well, so be it. I knew my girls had always loved my offbeat humor, so I tried it on my fellow "inmates," as I called us. It turns out that people with mental illness tend to have a quirky side! So my humor was well-received.

So even though my second stay in the mental hospital was for a whole month, and I had now lost two jobs, I left the second time feeling a bit more empowered. When I returned to the farm, I felt more resolved about Dick, and even apologized to him for declaring him the "devil" this time around. It actually became a kind of family joke for a while... our farm being the setting for the classic battle between good and evil, like a batman cartoon or a superman movie.

The truth is that I think I felt relieved to admit that I was mentally ill. They had changed my diagnosis this time from schizophrenia to manic depression. Even though I didn't know much about either, "my" illness sounded much less scary. I wasn't completely ready to admit that I had a permanent illness. I still suspected that this had happened because of stress. But I did know that something was not normal, and the new pills they gave me didn't have as many side effects, except water retention and weight gain. Apparently it was a "salt" that was in short supply in my system. Lithium. So when I took lithium, which is what they figured out at Ft. Logan, my moods evened out, and I would not get all manic and crazy. This sounded pretty good, too, because it made lithium sound more like a supplement than a medicine. Whatever. I came home with more bottles for the medicine cabinet.

After I came back, Dick talked to me about work. He said, "Wilma, why don't you take it easy for a while, instead of jumping back into work? I have a good-paying job now, and I can take care of the bills. You can just relax, and do some volunteer work for a while, maybe for R.S.V.P. even." I wasn't so sure about his idea of me going back and facing those ladies, and having to explain to them that I had just had a month-long dance with the crazies. But I did feel pretty tired, all around, and a little rest sounded nice to me.

I took on a few projects, here and there. Tried knitting and crocheting, and they both drove me crazy. Started up some painting again, did some silly animal paintings for the kids, and that was fun. I sometimes would take a drive up to Rocky Mountain Park, and would really enjoy walking around in the trees, and getting those long vistas over the valleys. The fresh air and the anonymity were good for me. But after a few months, I was starting to climb the walls.

That was when my sister called from British Columbia, and offered to pay for my ticket to come and see her. She and I had been close as kids, though she was ten years older. It turns out that she was dying of breast cancer, and she wanted to spend some time with her little sister again. I had once had a great vacation with her and a friend of hers,

Billie, in San Francisco. We had run around, bought big hats, and really enjoyed being "the girls" together. I guess I imagined a reprise of that experience---being able to "cut loose" a little and be myself with someone who really understood me. Dick had reservations about me taking a trip so soon after a hospitalization, but in the end, I won out, and the next thing I knew, I was on a plane for Seattle, with a connection for British Columbia.

Seeing my sister was more than I had bargained for. She was not the same woman I had played with 10 years before, by any stretch of the imagination. She was more shriveled, thin, and sickly. But most importantly, she was bitter. She made me look like Little Mary Sunshine! So it turned out that this visit was not to be me and my sister going on one last romp around town. She was too sick to go out for more than an hour or two at a time. Even though she was dying of breast and lung cancer, she was still smoking. She said to me jokingly, "Well, if I am going to go out anyway, I might as well go out with a puff of smoke!" I sighed deeply at that, and I realized that with all our craziness back on the farm, we had some things right in life. It could be that I was more put together, with my unemployment and hospitalizations, than my sister was, with her chainsmoking and cancerous thinking.

My nephews both lived in Victoria and Vancouver also, so they gave me some comic relief. My family had that Canadian/British type humor, and the conversational style that makes a conversation like one big, long sentence that everybody punctuates with their comments, and it was soothing to be with "my people" again, as a Canadian. It registered this time that Gil, my eldest nephew, had mental illness. It turned out that he had been diagnosed years ago with manic depression. He was the one who told me that it runs in families, and this revelation confused me. If it was me, then did that mean that it wasn't Dick? That didn't make any sense to me, so I tabled it for the time being. But I did like spending the time with Gil. We sort of "triggered" each other, and got really silly together. Then Wanda would come down on us both with her preachiness, and we would both turn on her and tease her a bit.

It was all going great, actually, and then one night Wanda got really, really sick. She coughed almost the whole night, and the next morning, her skin had an odd shade of almost green. She was in a really ill humor, and she suddenly reminded me of my mother, and reminded me of all those other things that I had forgotten. I started feeling kind of panicked, and then I realized that there were reasons for that, because there were men outside who were threatening all of us. I needed to warn Gil, before he came over, so I quickly told Wanda to "shut up!" and I called Gil, calling him "Deary" and speaking in code so that in case the men outside were listening, they wouldn't be in on my warning. Gil got kind of quiet, and then said, "Wilma, are you alright?" Then he came right over, and stayed with us for the whole day, and the next day too.

~~~ ∫∫ ~~~

On a soul level, Wilma began this chapter of her life with two leaps forward. First, she began to become self-aware. With that came a new humility and an appreciation for the condition of those around her. Remember that during her last hospitalization, she had felt completely and totally alone? This time, she began to look around. She stopped labeling the other patients around her as "losers," and began to see them each in their own individual human beauty. And when she was able to see them with compassion, she also was able to see and accept herself with more compassion. This was a huge step!

Wilma also began to develop gratitude during her second hospitalization. Instead of focusing on what was NOT there (job, stability, warm marriage relationship), she began to focus on what WAS there. Her children and husband were supportive of her. She had an environment in which she was beginning to learn more about herself and others. She found an avenue to give where she was. As the old adage goes, Wilma was learning to "bloom where she was planted."

While she was not reconciled with Dick, she was now able to view him with some perspective, and treat him with respect. She was even able to laugh at herself a little, and appreciate the role that humor played in her life. And did you notice that she now took a drive to the mountains *by herself* to find some peace and quiet, and reflect? She had learned, in some small way, to become more comfortable in her own skin. In the odd way that tragedy has of awakening the good in us, her last hospitalization had awakened new appreciation for her life, for nature, for her family, for the lives of the people that surrounded her. Wilma was no longer a child. She was growing up, internally. This was not scar tissue, but real healing.

The encounter with her sister was a harsh reminder of the world she had left behind when she left childhood. Her mother had died in a pool of bitterness, and that bitterness had been the poison that had killed the promise of her childhood. Remember that Wilma's mother had taught her independence, and that she had left her childhood home like a rocket, and had travelled as far away as she could, starting her adult life as a "rolling stone" that gathered no moss. After moving every two years in her young marriage, she had finally found a home in that rambling farm in Colorado, and had as few reminders of her childhood as possible, with her farm life, animals, open spaces, mountains, and a warm family.

Then, there before her, was another dying woman with her own bitterness, who reminded her of her family, her history, many of her dramas. Family members can often be a painful reminder of a painful past. Remember that Wilma had very few family ties, and those she had were weak enough. You might say that when she went to see her sister, she needed a home run, and what she got was a strike out.

The next chapter was possibly more painful for the rest of her family than it was for Wilma. While she was having the time of her life in manic bliss in British Columbia, Dick was receiving a call from Gil, telling him that Wilma had "gone off the deep end," and that he had better come and get her. Since putting her on a plane was out of the question, and they didn't want to get her trapped in the Canadian health care system, that left one option. Dick would have to take his girls out of school for a week, and drive up to British Columbia to fetch Wilma, and then somehow get her to come back to Colorado with them. It wouldn't be easy, but if he could enlist Mike's help, it would be possible. Shannon was in Oregon, which was kind of on the way, but since she had a young baby, he didn't want to mix it up too much there. Mike agreed, and they were off.

His daughters were quietly resentful about being pulled out of school. They were both very involved in school activities. He was vaguely aware that his youngest was on a debating team, and she was going to miss a meet. The older one was now accumulating accolades to get scholarships for college, and had two important meetings she would miss, plus a school newspaper deadline and a couple of choir rehearsals. He knew that they threw themselves into school as a way of coping with the confusion around the house, and that they no longer had friends come over for visits, since Wilma had.... Well, anyway, what had to be done had to be done, and there was no way that he could manage Wilma for 1,500 miles by himself.

Mike was much more cheerful about taking the break from college. He was almost too cheerful, and after several hundred miles of Mike's unflagging cheerfulness, he began to suspect that he son was high on something. Well, that was a battle for another day. For right now, what he needed to do was get Wilma.

There was one little blip on the trip up to get Wilma. They stopped for a lunch break on a beautiful beach in Oregon. The trees were ancient, and the old moss-covered trunks crumbled beneath your feet as you tried to walk on them. The beach was open and windswept, with some large and dramatic dark rock formations. Dick had his camera out and was taking pictures when he realized that Mike had been sitting in the same position for a very long time. He sent one of the girls over to check on him, and she came running back to tell him that Mike thought he was having a heart attack. His heart was not beating, and then beating very irregularly, he felt really dizzy and he wasn't sure he could stand. Dick went over, and Mike confessed that he had taken a pretty big hit of LSD, and he suspected that it had something else in it also. They dragged him to the car, and rushed their way to the hospital. On the way, his daughters nervously monitored his vital signs in the back seat. When they were almost to the hospital, something about the situation struck Mike as hilariously funny, and he started to laugh. When he kept laughing, and told everyone he felt fine now, Dick began to breathe easier, and they decided that they could skip the emergency room. It might be complicated anyway, if they had to divulge that Mike had been high on illegal drugs. Dick took a deep breath and kept his eyes on the road, as the girls giggled in the backseat at their brother's irrational laughter.

They made a quick pit stop at his daughter Shannon's place in Eugene, and went on to get Wilma. She was more than happy to join the road trip, and treated it all as a "lark," as she called it. They had to keep a sharp eye on her, to prevent her wandering off and saying something outlandish to someone, but the truth was that the trip was kind of fun. What was not so fun was when they had to tell her that the party was over, and she had to return to Ft. Logan. Everyone had decided that the care she got there was better, so it made more sense to have her return there. Plus, Poudre Valley would no longer take her, since Wilma was now showing herself to be chronically mentally ill, and Poudre Valley did not have the facilities to care for her properly.

At Ft. Logan, the rest of the family began to learn some small facts about the illness called manic depression. It was cyclical. Sometimes the cycles were very regular, and sometimes they were unexpected. The patient would cycle from periods of depression to periods of "mania," in which they would not sleep, would be hyperaware and hyperactive, sometimes combative and often delusional. The anti-psychotic drugs were the strong ones that treated the mania. Once she had stabilized, she could go back to a maintenance schedule of lithium. It was thought that manic cycles may be caused by stress, but no one really knew what caused manic depression. Oh, and there was one more fact. While schizophrenia tended to get better over the years, manic depression tended to get worse.

P'oesay Apyan:

It is hard for me to decide which of the periods of my life was the richest. Each shone with its own special beauty. No one can describe the joy one feels when his wife first places their precious baby in his arms, and he marvels at the beauty of Mother, to produce such divinity within all of us. And I experienced this five times in my lifetime.

And there were the years as a young man, when I was learning from my many fathers how to hunt, how to fish, how to create our shelters, how to learn to move with the cycles of the moon and the seasons, how to listen to the cries of our children, and of the animals in the forest, to learn what is happening or about to happen. All of nature has its seasons and its signals, to warn and prepare us for what is to come, if we listen carefully. When we listen carefully, we learn that all of creation sings the same song, and sometimes that helps us to make sense of situations that might otherwise confuse us.

It was like that when the white men first came to our valleys. We had many streams and forests. We harvested grains or flowers to eat that had grown wild around us, and after we harvested some of the fruit, the trees returned to bear fruit the following season. We took trees which were dead or nearly dead for our shelters, and the forest had not changed for lifetime upon lifetime.

Then one day, our elders heard the forest screaming. At first the cry was very soft, as if it was coming from many days away. The elders began to confer about the screams, and what they could mean. They turned to us, the young men, but we were not yet old enough to be able to hear the screams.

Then the birds began to arrive, and they were also moaning with disappointment. Their songs had changed, and even I could hear this change in the songs of the birds. We decided that we must move forward to attempt to find the source of the screams. We realized that we could follow the flight of the birds, and we would find it.

This was how we discovered the white man. He was using a metal ax, on a wooden handle, and was chopping down not one tree, as we would, to make a shelter on the forest floor. He was killing one tree sister after another, and laying their carcasses one on top of another, stripped of their leaves. We watched him quietly for weeks. He was unaware of our presence because he was unable to listen as we could. We wondered why he needed to take the lives of trees to build himself a shelter many, many times over. We did not realize then the white men preferred to live in "forts," which were tall structures with walls to keep out the red men like me. The coming of the white men was to teach me many lessons.

The first of these is that we do not know the things that we do not know. Inside of our hearts and our minds are our spirits, and up until this point, our spirits knew only the red man's ways. We had never seen a white man. We could not imagine the purpose for their towers, or how it was that they could not hear the trees screaming, or the reasons that they lived in fear of each other and of us. We could not know these things, because life gives us only some experiences, not all that is there to experience and know.

This is why we must always remain humble in life. We must always remember that a man has only two eyes--two windows through which he sees the world. When a man has a family, then he has many more eyes, and when he has a tribe, he has more eyes than he can ever see from all at one time. And when his spirit truly understands his relationship with our earth Mother, then he has an infinite number of eyes. I would never want to limit my vision to only one set of eyes.

Sometimes something magical has happened when I have looked into the eyes of another. I have looked inside his spirit or her spirit, and I have seen the life inside with all its beauty, just as if it were my own. When this happens, I feel warm appreciation for this other life, this sister or brother life that shares so many of my struggles and triumphs, yet is uniquely its own. I feel a deep sigh of contentment. It is as if my spirit has reached out and embraced the spirit of another. This is true happiness, to feel the connecting thread that weaves us all together into the beautiful tapestry of existence.

I look up to the Moon mother, and I give thanks for the seasons, and the tides of human life. Because our lives too have their cycles, their "seasons" of expansion and growth, and their seasons of darkness. When we begin to understand this interplay of the light with the darkness, then the darkness never will hold fear for us.

The weeks in the forest, watching the white man eliminate one tree mother after another, was one of those periods of darkness. We discussed this at night around our fire; we struggled to see into the soul of these white men, who apparently were deaf to the sounds that surrounded us daily. We knew now that we did not know, and some of us felt fear. But then the elders reminded us that Mother is always there, and the darkness always comes with light to guide our way. We needed only patience, and the path would reveal itself in time.

~~~ ʃʃ ~~~

CHAPTER SEVEN: ONE MORE TIME

≈ ≈ ≈ ≈ ≈ ≈ ≈ ≈ ≈ ≈ ≈ ≈ ≈ ≈ ≈ ≈ ≈

Wilma's Story:

The hospital was not as pleasant for me this time. For one thing, I felt perfectly normal when we got to the farm after the road trip, and all I wanted to do was rest there. The only problem was that when I tried to go to sleep, I didn't seem to be able to do it. So after laying there for what felt like hours, I would get up and start doing things around the house. Sometimes I would go in the kitchen and start to cook. Then one of the girls would come down the stairs groggily and say, "Please, Mom, I need to sleep. I have school tomorrow." For some reason, I would find that hysterically funny, and would try to coax the complaining kid to sit down and have a hot chocolate with me. If she did, I would start to tell her stories of my time with Wanda and Gil, and would be having a great time when Dick would come and break it up. He would literally say, "I need to break this up, Wilma. The girls need to get their sleep, and so do you." In an instant, my happy mood would turn to anger, and I would start to make fun of him, calling him a killjoy and a spoilsport. He would take it even-temperedly enough, but then I would start to feel like he was humoring me, not taking me seriously. It reminded me of the hospital, so I would tell him, "you are just like the idiot doctors, you have no idea what is really going on," and I guess I would run on and on.

At one point in one of these late night harangues, I looked over and realized that my littlest one was actually crying. She was just sitting there all slumped over on the chair, quietly sobbing to herself. This made me feel upset in a whole new way, that seemed to combine guilt and resentment and sadness and all sorts of emotions. I just stormed out of the room and went into the living room, on the other side of the house, and put on some classical music. I figured that the kids could sleep to that. Then I set about rearranging the books on the bookshelves. Dick came in and sat on the sofa and eyed me warily.

The next morning, after the kids were in school, Dick quietly told me he thought I needed to go back to the hospital until things quieted down a little, just to give the girls a little break. Something about the resignation in his voice made me feel sad along with him, and I agreed. They were such sweet girls. They really didn't need all this fighting around them. We left that morning for Denver.

Since this time I packed my own bag, I took things that I thought would be interesting, would spice things up at the hospital. I was in the mood for scarves, so I put a whole bunch of scarves in, and my mother's brooch, and a couple of my nicer outfits. Dick took note, and didn't comment. When we got to the hospital, he quietly took the brooch out of the bag. He knew it was one of the only things she had left me. Dick said it might not be safe in the hospital room, and "better safe than sorry." I didn't feel like fighting with him again.

So there it was again, in all its brown, concrete-walled glory: Ft. Logan. My third time here. This time was different yet again. I wasn't transported. I just walked in the door. They all seemed relieved that I wasn't as combative, so they didn't give me a heavy dose of anti-psychotics this time, so I was kind of perky. They showed me my room, Dick said goodbye, and then I looked around. I got restless in about five minutes, and headed out to make some trouble. The good thing about being in the mental hospital is that no one can really tell you to shut up. I mean they can give you drugs, but it's not like they will say, "Oh Wilma, stop acting crazy!" I mean, they expected me to act crazy, and that was kind of liberating. So I started bugging people. Mostly the orderlies, but sometimes the patients, too. This went well until the next morning, when they had me go in to see the psychiatrist. He glanced at me and scrawled a prescription, and within an hour or two I couldn't see straight. I think it must have taken me two days before I felt like doing anything, and that just made me mad. I had been so much better before I arrived than I was now!

So I decided to protest. In fact, I decided to organize a protest. The other patients weren't as game about it, but I did my best to rally them. I told them that we need to be treated better. I realized that I was a great leader, when I had a cause to support. I went back to my room and dressed up in my good clothes, and put on one of my brightest scarves, so that I could show even more leadership. The next thing I knew, three orderlies were on me, and they were shoving me into a room with a tiny window in a door that they slammed shut. Then the biggest one smiled at me through the tiny window, which had tiny threads of metal crisscrossing it. I was furious! I started to beat on the door and yell, but no one paid any attention. Then I looked around, and realized that there wasn't even a chair in there. It was a little room, 8 x 10 feet maybe, with white walls and absolutely nothing in it.

What was I supposed to do in here? I had gained a little weight, and I knew if I sat down on the floor, I wouldn't be able to get up. I paced around nervously for a while, like a caged animal. I was feeling very powerful, so much energy running through me, but what was this about now? This had never happened before. Finally, I returned to the door, and started staring through the little window at whoever walked by. I made faces. I screamed. I did anything I could to attract their attention. After a while, it was like I didn't exist anymore. They had tuned me out.

How long would I be in here? Can they *do* this? Is it legal? What would Dick think when he heard about it?

Well, Dick didn't hear about it, because I didn't see him for several days. I don't know how long I was in that room, but I was in high heels, and my feet started to hurt and swell. I took the shoes off. They still didn't come. It was dinner time, and no one came. Finally, they brought some food and some more pills, and made sure I took them. But they didn't take me out. I had no choice. I had to sit down, and once I did, I couldn't get up again. The pills always made me pee, but there wasn't a toilet in there. I was sure now that what they were doing was not legal. I hated Ft. Logan. I sat there and peed in my pants, and then waited for them to take me out.

Needless to say, my love affair with Ft. Logan was over now. I was at war. They would drug me, and as soon as the drugs started to wear off, I would start to fight with them. It was the only thing I could do to preserve my dignity, to convince myself that they hadn't won. I don't remember seeing my family for days. I think they told them to stay away. Plus the girls could only come on the weekends, because of school. The weeks were interminable. The therapy seemed useless. No one seemed to care. The world was an incredibly hostile place, and the only thing that kept me going was knowing that one day I would be able to walk out of that place and never cast eyes on it again.

It would be almost four months this time before I made it out of Ft. Logan. By the time I left, the feeling was mutual, and we were told that I would not be allowed to return. It became a little bit of a family joke, Mom's war against the mental hospital. But the truth was that it wasn't funny. One time my daughters came to see me while I was in the "pen." One of them must have insisted that they show her where I was, and the older one's face suddenly appeared in the tiny, one-foot by one-foot window, eyes wide with horror. I must have looked a sight. I was back in a hospital robe, because of the absence of a toilet in the room, I guess. Easier to clean. I am sure that my hair had not been combed in days. When I saw her, I ran over to the other side of the glass, and tried to talk to her. All I could hear was a muffled sound, and I realized that the room was soundproofed. I was crying really hard now, and kept repeating to her over and over, mouthing it so she would understand, "Get me out of here! You have to get me out of here!" She was crying too, and I could see that she was telling me that she would, and she walked away quickly, and I never saw her again that night.

I guess she was not able to do anything. No. It wasn't really very funny at all.

But I will say that it was quite a while before I was hospitalized again. I would say it was about a year and a half. During that time, a lot of things happened. My eldest had her second child, and moved back from Oregon. She now lived in the mountains outside of Loveland, where we lived. She was thinking about going back to college in nearby Fort Collins. My middle daughter graduated. My son quit college and moved to Alma, Colorado, the highest incorporated town in the United States, and started living with some other hippy friends of his, studying eastern religion and minoring in drugs, I suspected, while he worked construction. My youngest daughter was tied for valedictorian of her high school class, was a senior member of the debate team, was in school plays, and was continuing her religious interests. The middle daughter had abandoned fundamentalism after a trip she had taken to Germany, to see some Lutheran nuns she had met in Denver at a retreat. She had worked at a boatyard on a lake over the first two months of the summer, and then used the money to travel the third month, during the summer after her sophomore year. I was so proud of her, and arranged for her to fly with some others who were attending the Lutheran conference with her. It turned out that she ditched them and came back on her own a month later, with a glowing report of her experiences of Germany, Austria, and Switzerland. I was especially proud because she had made it to Europe at 15, and I had still never been!

The youngest outdid her sister, though. She joined a missionary effort, raised the funds to send herself, and went to Colombia for four weeks to work in the jungle building a school, with Teen Missions, after her sophomore year. What drive! She also came back with glowing reports, and continued to excel in school.

I wasn't particularly productive, but I kept busy, keeping up with what the kids were doing, feeding all the pets, and occasionally visiting the mother of one of my daughter's best friends, Jeanne Lamb. Jeanne was an unusual woman, and for some reason she had taken a shine to me. She was a junior high science teacher, a career woman, who had married an alcoholic at 18, had three kids, and then managed to pull herself together, divorce the guy, and raise the three kids on her own, while getting herself through college. She was extraordinary. A very hard woman, much feared by her students and her kids, to hear my daughter tell it. But then life had not been easy on her, so I understood how that could happen.

What was nice was that Jeanne had ended up meeting a chemistry teacher, a big strapping good-looking guy, a few years her junior, and they had gotten married. And Jeanne had become much softer, lighter, and more fun to be around. And Chris was also a nice guy. They built a solar house in the country five or ten miles away, and Chris built airplanes from kits as a hobby, while they continued to improve their house and make it energetically self-sufficient. They were interesting people, and I had a friend.

I think that Jeanne didn't think much of Dick, but she tolerated him. She knew he was a hands-off parent, and not really good for much for me either, except for bringing home a paycheck. But she did respect that he had stuck with me through all these hospitalizations. Jeanne had never seen me when I was loopy, and I didn't elaborate. I really wanted to keep her respect.

Jeanne also encouraged me to leave Dick. She said I could support myself without him. She had done it, and so could I. I told her I wasn't going to make any moves while the girls were still at home. But Erin was finally graduating, and had decided that notwithstanding her almost perfect grade point average, she was going to be a missionary instead of a college student, and she shipped off to Scotland of all places, to help run a school there. Kelley was in her second year of college, and was having a blast at the University of Colorado, about one hour away. I was spending time babysitting for the grandkids, and Dick was staying out of my way. Mike had decided to join some guru from India and had moved into Denver and had a really nice girlfriend. He came to visit fairly frequently. So overall, things were looking up.

And I think that Ft. Logan had finally put the fear of God into me, and I was taking my pills "religiously," if you don't mind the pun. But that was about all the religion I could muster these days. Something about that last visit to Ft.

Logan had made me cynical about God and religion. I suspected that we did not have any magical power to call upon God through prayer to save us. After all, I had called out to God plenty during those days I was in the "pen," prayed in Jesus name, did everything. The kids always made sure I had a Bible by my bed. But....nothing. That is what I got back from the Almighty Creator, for all my efforts. A big fat nothing.

I kept my thoughts to myself, except with Mike, who was pretty open-minded, and not as judgmental as the others. After all, remember that Dick was a born-again, Erin was a missionary, Kelley was quiet these days about her beliefs, and Shannon had also joined the bandwagon, and was now a Seventh Day Adventist. With Mike following an Indian guru, we had quite the spiritual covey at our house, so being an atheist or even an agnostic was not something that would be well-received.

During those last months when Erin was finishing school, I was quietly making my own plans now, to be revealed after her graduation. I was going to move to Estes Park, and get a job there!

~~~ ∫∫ ~~~

So what was happening this time to Wilma, in her times of adversity and the aftermath? Several things had been changing in her during these years. You might notice that she had begun to "rage against the machine" again, had recovered some of her spunk. She could now jokingly refer to herself as a "Looney," and the idea was not as depressing as it had been before. She had now accepted the idea that she had a mental illness, and needed medication, and she had finally stabilized. With all the support in her surrounding environment, things were going pretty well.

And after all these years, Wilma was stepping forward, with the encouragement of her new friend, to create her own life. She had defined herself by her mother's criticism, then by her husband's rejection, then by her children's needs, and now, finally, she was about to define herself on her own terms. Wilma was ready to explore her own identity, much in the same way that Dick did, when he took his epic journey to Russia, which had ended in disappointment. Wilma was continuing in this belated process of growing up, assisted by the constant challenge of her mental illness. She was learning.

P'oesay Apyan:

There is a deep place within us, and when we find that place, we cannot be removed by anyone or anything. It took me many years to find that place, but I did find it in my third decade on the earth. My children were growing, and the tribe was thriving. I was no longer turning to the elders every time I needed guidance. I was beginning to turn inside myself first, and go to others after only to see what they might have to add.

Others had noticed my assurance, and had begun to come to me for advice. This was a surprise to me at first, but after a time, I recognized that I too trusted my own counsel above others. I was young, but was treated as an elder, and it became clear to everyone that I was the appropriate choice for Chief of my people.

With this position came much responsibility. When the tribe faced a crisis, the Chief was the one who would make the final decision on which path to take. And for my tribe, the role of the Chief was particularly challenging, because the white men had not gone away. The first one had been followed by others, and there was now a large colony there where the fort had first been constructed. At first they had confined themselves within the walls, but it appeared that their appetites were insatiable, and they kept on taking more and more of the tree mothers, expanding the scar upon the land, and causing the cries of the birds and other creatures. In fact, we were now so accustomed to those cries that we hardly heard them anymore. The white men left us to our own devices, but many in the tribe were becoming angry at them. At first, we had decided that we could simply let them take their space and we would continue to go about our lives as usual.

But they kept on coming. Every spring, another group of 30 or 40 would arrive, and even more would continue heading toward the setting sun. They were spreading over the landscape like ants, but ants that carried fire power, and still hated and feared the red man. We did our best to avoid them, to stay hidden in the forest, and to hunt in areas where they could not find us. But we heard tales from our brothers of massacres, whenever the red man and the white man attempted to cross paths. We knew that the time was coming when we would have to have a confrontation with the white man, and I did not know how that confrontation would go. I did not want to spill the blood of even one of my people. Each of them I had known since birth, theirs or mine, and they were all my family, were one with me. I could not spare one life, in the struggle with the white man. I spent much time in contemplation, attempting to listen to earth Mother and hear her advice. And I waited for the time when I would need to step forward, as the voice of my people, and ask the white man to join hands with us in being the keepers of the Earth.

I knew that we had a lesson to share with the white man. I could see from observing them at work that they did not feel the life in the earth beneath them, as we did. They walked with hard gaits, on hard shoes, and they did not pause in their daily activities to listen to the birds or hear the breeze, or look up at the expanse of sky above us and sigh with gratitude. Their eyes were always cast down, focused on their work, work, work. This is how my people came to give them the name of "Ant People."

Sometimes, when I sat in the quiet of the night and looked up at the moon, I knew that a time of great change was coming for my people. And I felt that this change would not be an easy one for any of us. But for now, all I could do was wait.

~~~ ∫∫ ~~~

CHAPTER EIGHT:
SPREADING MY WINGS

≈≈≈≈≈≈≈≈≈≈≈≈≈≈≈≈≈≈≈≈≈≈≈≈

Wilma's story

I am sorry to bring you more bad news, but I did it again. Erin had just graduated and was on her way to missionary training, and Kelley had a conference in California. She was involved in politics at the college in Boulder, and was the chairwoman of several committees, including the University Planning Commission, so in that capacity, she would represent the University at this conference in San Francisco. I still had fond memories of San Francisco, so I suggested that I go along with her, and we drive my car. To my surprise, she enthusiastically agreed. We also had enjoyed some camping trips, just the girls and I, during the time that Dick was away in New England, and travelled pretty well together. I was ecstatic to have this time to have her all to myself. So as soon as Erin shipped off to training in Florida for a year, Kelley and I hit the road.

At first it went great. We sang songs, stuck our feet out the windows, talked about life. I told her stories of Wanda and me and the fun we had in San Francisco. It is a 24 hour drive from Colorado to the west coast, through some of the most beautiful and stunning country that America has to offer. The highway also passed through Salt Lake City, where my husband and I were married, so I told Kelley that story again, as we passed through. When we got to the salt flats, maybe 100 miles of pristine white flats of dried mud, lined by distant mountains, it was sunset, and the flats were tinted orange with the setting sun, and this same sun somehow turned the mountains to a deep lavender, and the sky to soft green. She asked if we could pull over, along the "gun-barrel" highway that cut through the middle of the flats. I agreed, and we pulled off onto the shoulder, and walked out into this desert of all deserts, where nothing grows at all. The dried mud separated into jigsaw puzzle pieces with curled corners, all fitted perfectly together into a mosaic that extended to the horizon. It was spectacular. I looked up and saw that Kelley had walked far out into the flats. She probably wanted to get as far from the highway as she could, so that she could pretend that nothing existed but the sky, the rim of mountains, and the white, flat expanse of clay. When a moment later she laid down on her back on the flats, gazing up at the sky, I knew I was right, and I did the same.

We were very excited when we finally got to the "left coast." Since we lived in an area that was landlocked, the ocean was always a marvel. We arrived there late in the day, too, and pulled over at the first opportunity, to walk out to a point of land overlooking the ocean from the top of sharp, dark-colored stone cliffs. This was when our first problem arose. Kelley fearlessly walked out on one of the fingers of cliff, and stood at the edge, looking down at the ocean. I watched her in the evening light, and thought, "I can do that too!" I picked another finger of land, and strode out on it with confidence. I got near the edge, and there was small step down of maybe a foot or two, onto a little platform of maybe 5 or 6 feet square. After that square of safety, the cliffs plunged straight down to the swirling waves on the rocks a thousand feet below.

Once I was there, and I saw that drop off, I had second thoughts about my idea. I was a little heavy, with all the lithium capsules and water weight, and that ocean was really scary. I panicked a little, and turned to return to safety. But now that foot and a half of ledge seemed insurmountable to me. I panicked some more, and started to call out to Kelley, who was still looking out over the view from the point to my right, self-absorbed. At first she ignored me, over the roar of the surf below us. Then she turned and derisively called, "Come on, Mom! You can climb that!" When I told her I was scared to try, and I wanted her to come and take my hand, she just repeated, "You can do it. Just turn around and sit down, then swing your feet onto the ledge beside you and get up!"

I am sure that it looked easy to a 20 year old, but for this top-heavy old lady, I could see all sorts of things going wrong, and I felt worse than panicked. I felt abandoned. All of the sudden, the beautiful trip felt all wrong. My daughter was annoyed with me. I was an annoyance, and she didn't want me there. On top of that, I couldn't take care of myself, and she didn't want to help me, so I was on my own, just as I was every time I went into that stinking hospital.

I don't know how to describe it, but the pressure in my head was enormous. It was like my thoughts started screaming at me, and I was miserable. I started to cry. When she finally came and helped me off the little ledge, her contempt was palpable, and we rode the rest of the way to San Francisco in silence. I felt crushed.

San Francisco was fun, though the blush was off the rose for me. I could see that Kelley felt guilty and kept trying to make it up to me, but my mood had shifted, and now I felt brooding most of the time. The party at the end of her conference was fun though, and I was glad to see that she didn't completely shun me as she made the rounds with the bigwigs of the conference. I was proud of her self-assurance, and wondered where she had gotten it from. Sometimes it was hard to believe that these were my children, all grown up..... The same kids I used to hold on my knee while I spoon-fed cereal into their open mouths. Life was too fast, the moments were so bright and glorious, and then they passed and were gone, and this also depressed me. Finally, I left the party and returned to the hotel room to wait for her. I knew she would be relieved to not be "escorted" by her mother, and to appear as an independent young lady again.

On the way back from California, my depression turned to euphoria, and I became more and more enthused as the miles of road whizzed beneath us. I started talking to Kelley about everything, telling her things my brother Warren and I had done together when we were kids, and what I could remember of Saskatchewan. Then it was my work, and the farm, and the plans we had had for it in the beginning, and...... Finally, Kelley said wearily, "Mom, would it be okay if we just rode in silence for a while, and listened to the radio?" For some reason this really offended me, and I turned to the window in a huff. But a little while later, something would occur to me, and I would be at it again. We made it back in one piece, but Kelley looked pretty beat. She had done most of the driving. When we got to the farm, I saw her go outside with Dick for a few minutes to have a private conversation, and I got a feeling of foreboding. Oh no. It can't be. Not now, when my youngest has just graduated, my grandkids are toddlers, my boy is doing so well, and my middle daughter is a BWOC..... And not now, just when I was going to spring my surprise on everyone, and move to Estes Park!

Estes Park was this small town tucked into an open mountain valley about 45 minutes' drive from Loveland. When the kids were growing up, it was always a favorite stop for us on our way into Rocky Mountain National Park. Rocky Mountain Park had the highest concentration of peaks over 14,000 in the U.S., outside of Alaska, and really was spectacular. We would go there every Fourth of July since we had landed in Colorado, and eat a picnic lunch next to a bubbling mountain stream that roared steeply over the rocks down the canyon, and out onto the valley floor, where we lived. There was the pine scent, the wildflowers, the birds.... I loved the Park. And Estes Park was the place we stopped on the way to buy homemade taffy or fudge, and walk the old fashioned streets and stretch our legs before making the last leg of our journey. It was a small place, full of happy memories, and I felt like I knew it like the back of my hand. It was the perfect place for me to make a fresh start, and I had heard about a job up there that might suit me. Someone from the Chamber of Commerce had told me that Shirley at a local visitors' bureau was going to retire soon. The pay was very poor, but enough to live on.

But unfortunately, it looked like I was headed for the hospital again.

Yes, this process was getting easier every time now, but I was not at all sure that this was a good thing. What if the hospitalizations continued until all the fight was taken out of me? Who would I be then? I had to make it to Estes Park. I had to show all of them that I could do this; I could make it on my own, show all of them what I was made of.

While they were talking, I grabbed the keys and headed out the other door for the cars. Dick intercepted me as I reached the car door, and grabbed my key hand under his big one and held on. A fight ensued, but he was much stronger. Eventually, he wrested the keys from my hands, which were now red from the struggle. I sunk to the ground right there on the gravel of the driveway, and started to cry. What else was there to do? My middle daughter sat there next to me, and took my hand in hers and rubbed it gently. The tears were pouring out of me now like buckets. I didn't want to be weak in front of her. I wanted to be strong. I wanted to make her proud of me, to get my apartment, to start my new life! All of this just made me cry harder, made me even more the blubbering, weak idiot that I already was.

I eventually stopped crying. The sun had gone down, and in the plains, even in the summer, when the sun sets the ground starts to get cold. We went in, and I insisted on making everyone dinner. It was my old favorite, tuna casserole. The three of us ate a hearty portion each, and I did feel a little better. Kelley helped me pack that night, and the next day, they both drove me to the hospital. We were all pretty quiet. I think it had dawned on us that this had started to become a routine.

It turned out that, lucky us, there was another mental hospital in Denver, since I was a *persona non grata* at Ft. Logan. This time they took me to a small regional hospital, where the nurses were gentle and the patients appeared more senile than crazy. Of course, this was a relief, but I actually wondered if they would be able to handle me. Turns out that I had nothing to worry about on their account. Their philosophy was, when in doubt, increase the dosage! So within hours of my arrival, it was dreams, sweet dreams. I have no idea when I woke up, but I know that I couldn't talk at all. I literally could not form words with my mouth. My hands immediately went to my mouth, to see if there was something over it, and then I groggily pulled myself to the mirror to stare into my own face, puzzled. All the parts were there. But when I tried to formulate a word, when my mind told me to create the shape for a sound to emerge, my jaws just remained where they were, flaccid. I went to find a pad and paper, and scrawled out a question to the nurse. My handwriting was not much better than my mouth, but at least I got something down, after much effort.

I made my way out to the nursing station, with my note, which read, "Whats wrong I can't talk!" The nurse looked at me sweetly, and said, "Oh no, don't worry, Wilma. That's just the side effects of the Haldol. Why don't you go sleep it off?" She then smiled at me, and returned to her paperwork.

Haldol. This was the second time that I really paid attention to the names that they gave the drugs they pumped me full of. I knew lithium, of course, since I took it daily, most of the time. (I had run out on the California trip, but didn't want to tell Kelley, since things were going so well.) And it seemed like there was a battery of different types of drugs they would give me when I was hospitalized. But this Haldol.... why did they keep giving it to me if it did this?

I had to admit that my restless mind was certainly quiet. It seemed to take minutes to formulate a complete thought. It was all just too exhausting, and I went back to bed. The next time I woke up, a nurse was bathing me with a washcloth, there in the bed, and then she propped me up on some pillows and helped me eat some food (not so easy when a person's mouth won't close without a hand manually shutting it between each bite!) and then she gave me more pills and eased me back to bed, all with that perennial smile. I tried to muster some sort of sarcastic comment for her, but it was just too much effort. I felt like I was half dead. As I drifted off to sleep again, I wondered how many of those patients I had seen when I came in were actually senile, and how many were just drugged to within an inch of their lives, like I was. Then I was out again.

Kelley came a few days later to visit. She said that Mike had come several times, and Dad and Shannon, too, but I was always sleeping. She said that Mike would be able to visit me more often this time, since he lived in Denver also. I was still lying stretched out in my bed, and my muscles felt pretty sore. I'll bet I wasn't out of that bed more than 15 minutes, all told, in the last week. But at least my mind was somewhat clear, though I still couldn't talk.

She looked in my eyes questioningly, and asked me if I could understand what she was saying. I nodded my head vigorously, and tried to smile. She saw the effort, and appeared relieved. She said, "Mom, I have something to tell you. I have decided to quit school and move to New York City. Remember that I went there last Christmas break with Suzanne and Randy? Well, you know that I really loved it, and Randy is in school at NYU, so it's not like I won't know anyone there, but I really feel like I need to do this. School just seems stale, and I want to experience more of life. So I am going to take some time off, and maybe I will go back next year."

Oh my God. No, please, don't come to me when I can't even talk, and drop a bombshell like that! I need to tell you to stay in school, that things are going well, you have friends, you have a future. Now I have one daughter who graduated valedictorian who skipped college to be a missionary, another who quit college to have babies, a son who quit to follow a guru, and this one who had seemed to have it together was quitting to do nothing at all? *I* needed to do something; I needed to tell her........ What?

Look at me, lying here flat in a hospital bed, so drugged up that I literally can't even wish her good luck. What kind of advice would she want to take from someone in my position? My eyes filled with tears of helplessness and frustration. She misunderstood, and said, "Oh, no, Mom, don't cry. I will come back soon to visit. I promise I will be back for Christmas. It is just something I want to do, to experience life in the big city, you know, the Big Apple, and all. It is just so different, and there is so much I can learn there......"

I tried to wipe my eye, but my arms weren't much better than my mouth, so she took a tissue and wiped my eyes, and we both cried there together, her with her head on my stomach, holding my hand in hers. There wasn't much to say, really. What a difference two weeks makes, I thought, remembering the jubilant launch of our California adventure. And then she was gone.

After Kelley left, it dawned on me that all my children were gone. Erin had left for Florida a couple weeks before, now Kelley was leaving within days. Mike and Shannon had left years before. And I was becoming an old woman fast. It made everything look different, somehow. I really needed to think about things.

And to do that, I needed to get off these drugs! I started writing notes to the nurses to please reduce my dosage. A doctor came in once and glanced at me, and left the nurse with a little piece of paper. And within a few days after Kelley had left for New York City, I could talk again. But this time, instead of giving anyone a piece of my mind, I laid low, didn't say much of anything, and when Dick came,

I asked him to ask them if I could go home again. I wasn't delusional or dangerous to myself or anybody else, was I? Apparently, the doctors agreed, and within 3 weeks (in record time, for me) I was released from that little hospital, a free woman again.

I came back to the farm much subdued. I think Dick liked me better when I was feisty, fighting people, speaking my mind, even putting him down. That was what he was used to now. But I had a lot of thinking to do. First, I was going to stick to those meds like glue. I needed to keep it together long enough to make it to Estes Park. I started walking a little in the mornings, just around the farm, to lose some of this water weight, and tried to eat more sensibly. I made a couple of phone calls. The job was still open. All I had to do was get a little stronger, and I would set out to Estes Park, to see what I could find out.

~~~ ∬ ~~~

So what was happening at this point in Wilma's story? In her last trip to the hospital, she had been raging against life, finding people to blame for her predicament, and expending all of her hard-won energy fighting anyone she could. Remember that Wilma had come into adulthood with the heart and emotions of a child, with what you might call an incomplete package. Intellectually and creatively, she could hold her own. But she had never really developed a solid sense of her own identity. And a little like a three year old, she lashed out at others when she did not get her own way. When she was angry, she did not care whose fault anything was, as long as there was someone to blame. First it was Dick, then her boss, and then it was the hospital employees. She saw life as hostile, and she had declared war.

And just as a child at first becomes empowered by his anger, by the realization that he can break things, and then later realizes that by breaking things, he has only hurt himself, it had begun to dawn on Wilma that the person who needed to take care of her was herself. At the moment that her daughter rebelled against becoming the caretaker of her mother, on that cliff in California, Wilma was also facing a stark realization: She was not a child anymore, and there wouldn't always be someone who would step forward to take care of the problems she had created.

Before she had felt helpless, as if there was nothing she could do but wait for someone or something to rescue her. She cried out to God, to no avail, to her family, to no avail, to the hospitals, to no avail. And through all of that, she came to a sobering conclusion: "There is no one left to wait for. I am on my own in this." Wilma moved from feeling helpless to recognizing her role in what happened. But she felt very, very weak. Her point of greatest weakness coincided with this most recent hospitalization, in which she was deliberately drugged to keep her weak and to avoid becoming a problem to the other patients, or to the facility. And she realized that she needed to create a strategy, to get herself out of that helpless position. She needed to rise from this half-dead state, resurrect herself, and begin a new life. Ironically, she was at the beginning stages of the "new birth" experience that had eluded her in her fundamentalist explorations.

She was on her way to a new life.

P'oesay Apyan:

I had reached my 40th year now. People were beginning to refer to me as a "great Chief" of my people. I found this ironic, since it appeared that my wisdom came from admitting what I did not know. I did not know where the Ant People would stop, in their advance against the red man, in their devouring of the landscape. I did not know how our people could contest them, without losing the lives of our loved ones, of our sister souls. It seemed to me that I raised far more questions than I answered, but other tribes were now sending emissaries from far away to come and speak with me about the blight of the white man upon our lands. We heard that they had advanced all the way to the Great Water now, and were concentrated there, attempting to pull the treasures of gold and silver from the earth.... those that our brothers from the south had melted into small objects to honor their sun gods, the rain gods, and even Earth Mother. They concentrated in large villages now, which spotted the whole countryside.

My own tribe had now moved far into the mountains, to avoid the Ant People, and we now had to scratch out a living in cold air, and face the cold winters while the mild valley lay before us, scarred now from the Ant People's insatiable hunger to kill the tree mothers. Our forests were disappearing, and the deer had also left for the high country. But we could no longer collect our wild grains, either, and life was becoming more and more difficult for our tribe, as each spring more and more Ant People appeared on the horizon in their long strings, always marching, marching toward the setting sun.

I think that the others came to me because I always gave the same counsel. I always told every emissary that I could not permit the blood of one of my loved ones to flow, because of the hate of the Ant People. I explained how all the red men are One, and that when one dies, we all feel that touch of death. I explained that we are all one Body, and that we need each person, just as the body cannot function well without hands, without legs, without eyes. We needed to continue to see the world through the many eyes of our tribe, and to eventually teach the white men to also see through the many eyes. Since we were all of one Spirit, if we were to send some of our tribe to kill the white men, we would be killing our own souls. I explained that if the body dies, the soul will live on, but if we send a body to its death, then we kill our own tribal Spirit, and we needed to remain strong, to face the white men with our Spirit heart intact.

Many others did not like my counsel. They were filled with anger, and they wanted to fight. They said that we needed to eliminate the white men, while our numbers were still greater than theirs. They said that with each year that we delayed, the task became bigger, and if we waited too long, we were destined to fail. They said that Earth Mother had left the red man in her charge, that it fell upon us to protect Mother from harm, and that the white man did not understand Mother, and was killing her. They said that if we did not fight now, we were failing Mother.

But I reminded them that the Ant People had firepower, and we did not. With one stick of firepower, one white man could kill many red men. Much blood would flow, and the white men would retreat to their forts, behind tall walls where our arrows could not touch them. They responded, "Then more must come and fight. We must capture the white man's firepower, and use it against him."

When they said this, I looked into the future, and I saw a world in which one man stood with firepower against another man, and the other man stood with his own firepower, pointed at the first. I saw lines of these men, facing each other, and as they fired, many fell, and much blood was lost. I saw families falling into small pieces, and tribes being decimated, with no one left to care for the old or for the children. And worst of all, when I saw this scene, I could not tell which was the white man and which was the red man. The red man had become so much like the white man that he had become him, and the red man was no more. His soul had been silenced. This is the danger of a life lived in anger: the good inside a man is destroyed.

But what I told those who argued for war was more simple. I said it was a war that could never be won, in which all would lose---Mother, the red man, and the white man too. The fighting would end, yes. But the voice of Mother, the voice of Spirit, would be forever silenced. When the last of us fell, Mother would have lost her voice. We needed to keep her voice alive. This was more important than winning any battle.

I could see these visions, yes. But what was Mother telling me to do? So I sat with my family. My sons were growing strong, and some had already taken a wife. We learned new ways to create shelters, new ways to hunt. And as we were moved deeper and deeper into the mountains, the villages on the plains, and in the hills that bordered these mountains, became larger and larger. What had begun as one fort that we had watched be constructed years ago was now a large village that expanded far beyond the edges of the fort where it had begun, and a new fort had been built to control the red men. Other villages were spreading all over the plains where we had once hunted. The emissaries came and told us that, though the hostilities continued, some of the tribes were trading furs and blankets at this new fort.

~~~ ∫∫ ~~~

CHAPTER NINE:
A NEW PAGE

≈ ≈ ≈ ≈ ≈ ≈ ≈ ≈ ≈ ≈ ≈ ≈ ≈

Wilma's story:

I waited a week or two before I went up to Estes Park. I knew that I never looked good after a hospital visit, and with this one, I had been so pumped full of drugs that my face looked like ash when I got out, and it even seemed like parts of my face still weren't responding to show my expressions normally. I took walks with the dogs, got some fresh air, and sunbathed in the back yard, and got some color back in my face. I went to visit Jeanne, and told her what I was planning. She was ecstatic for me, and her big smile really encouraged me. It was nice to know I had a real friend, after all these years.

I didn't tell Dick about my plans. I knew there was really nothing he could say. After all, how many times had he taken off? I just didn't want to take a chance on anyone weakening my resolve. This was the time to make my move, and I was going to make it!

And it all went great. I called and made an appointment. They liked my Chamber experience and my work with volunteers at R.S.V.P. They asked what I had been doing lately, and I told them I had taken time off due to health issues, and they did not press for details. I was in!

My next step was finding a place to live. Believe it or not, this was a first for me, at 52 years old. When I worked for the sororities as a traveling salesperson, at first I stayed at my mother's when I was in town, and later I moved into a rooming house, because I was in town so seldom. Essentially, I had lived out of a suitcase until I got married, and since then, of course I was with the family. I was finally getting a taste of the excitement that the kids experienced when they set out for a new place, to start a new life. Somehow, this step made me feel closer to them.

I found a beautiful tiny apartment, on the second floor of a retailer on a side street, right off the main drag. But it had a little window which looked out on Main Street and beyond Main Street to the open valley that gave the town its name. A "park" in mountain terms is a wide valley in the middle of tall mountains, and Estes Park was one of the biggest in this part of the state, which hosted a large man-made reservoir, used to control runoff flowing down the

Big Thompson Canyon, which fed right into good old Loveland. It was this same water that was fed into the little spiders of irrigation ditches that watered our farm. Water was a funny thing in Colorado. The mountains could get 30 to 60 inches of precipitation a year, and most of it snow. Above Estes Park was Trail Ridge Road, which actually had been used sometimes by the settlers to go over the mountains on their way to California, because it was big, gradual, and bald, since it went above tree line. But that was only in the summer, because in the winter, the road was buried under 30 feet of snow.

But the plains down below, which we looked out upon from our mountain perch, received only 10 inches of precipitation a year, most of it snow. 10 inches is the same as the deserts in New Mexico and Arizona receive, just to our south. What this meant is that our verdant green valley was only green because of the crisscrossing irrigation ditches that fed all this clean mountain water to the farms and ranches that dappled the countryside. There were some natural lakes here and there, especially in the foothills, which were still forested and stayed green longer with the runoff from the mountains. But the valley was all farms and ranches, in that checkerboard pattern that reflected how all the land had been given out to the settlers, back in the days when Colorado was being settled. The U.S. government divided the whole country up into ugly squares, and then handed them out to anyone who wanted them.

So, though I was only three-quarters of an hour from the outskirts of Loveland here, I was in a completely different world. Up here, the air was crisp and cold in the morning, even in the summer. The mountains were teeming with life, and Rocky Mountain Park even still had herds of Big Horn Sheep, which were able to walk straight up those rocky mountain faces as if they were taking a stroll in the park (which, in fact, they were)!

I loved my new job. I sat at a desk all day and greeted visitors as they came in, and told them interesting facts about the history of the state, and features of the National Park. I also managed to throw in a little lore about local ghost stories and information about the gold rush. It was much easier than my Chamber job had been, but then I was ready for easy, which my life had decidedly not been in the last few years. And speaking of easy, it had almost been too easy to convince Dick that I wanted to move to Estes Park. He just asked me, "Wilma, are you sure you can handle it?" And from my glare in response, I think he was convinced not to question me again.

I didn't take too much with me, because I didn't need much, and not too much would fit in my postage stamp of an apartment, anyway. I wasn't sure if I would ever return to the farm. I wasn't sure that I wanted to say goodbye, either. It had been such a haven for me, and I missed the pets, especially the horses. Their big, hulking presences always made me feel safe. Since Dick and I had not even shared a bedroom for at least ten years now, it wasn't like we really got into each other's way. But Estes Park was literally a breath of fresh air, and I felt like my whole soul was awakening. Each day was better than the last.

The best part was that during my free time, in ten minutes I could be walking on a path in Rocky Mountain National Park. My favorite place was the spot where the family used to have our Fourth of July picnics. The road wound all through the huge open park, and then wound up some steep switchbacks at the other end, back and forth until I was looking out over the whole Front Range, and Denver was just a speck in the distance, blurred by the smog that sat over the plains. The parking lot sat between a lovely little mountain lake and the stream, which was lined with picnic tables.

Sometimes I would take a little "picnic dinner" with me, and sit in the spot where the family always used to set up each year. I would listen to the sound of the water rushing over the rocks, and watch the birds flitting through the trees. During the summer, all the migrating birds came back, and the trees were alive with them. One day, as I sat at the table listening, one of them flitted down and landed right next to me on the table. I was startled at first, but it seemed the bird was as curious about me as I was about it. I extended the index finger of my hand, which was resting on the table, and wouldn't you know it? The little thing hopped over, and then after a moment of hesitation, hopped onto my finger as if it were a stick! Then it seemed to immediately realize its mistake, and flew away. But what a magical moment.

I enjoyed walking near the lake the most. There was a trail along the edge, that got a little marshy in places, and no one really came over here, since there were no picnic tables. I would put on the moccasins I had purchased at one of the Estes Park tourist traps on a splurge, and make my way along the path as quietly as I could, so as not to disturb the nature that I encountered. Mostly there were insects along the path, which, I am sure, attracted the birds, but once in a while, I would see the smooth skin of an otter in the water, or find a little turtle on the water's edge. I wished we had explored this side more when the kids were little. I imagined bringing them here when they came to visit me in my new home. Now I could bring my grandkids! In fact, Shannon and her brood did come up and visit me in my new place. My granddaughter Willow looked at me with her wide eyes and said, "Grandma, this place is great!" and my heart swelled with happiness. When I looked in the mirror these days, I could see myself again. I hated the sight of that small box of pills on the counter each morning, but I took them. It was the price I had to pay for Paradise.

~~~ ∫∫ ~~~

Wilma had discovered the truth in that old adage, "To thine own self be true." She had realized that the way she had been living before, even though she was completely devoted to her family, wasn't serving anyone at all, because she herself had been miserable. Eventually, the force of all that misery had come crashing down on her, sent her into a tailspin, and left her reeling with no place to turn. And at that critical juncture in her life, she had made a good choice. She had looked at herself hard in the mirror, and she had turned inside. She had realized that she, too, had choices, just like her children, and though the odds were against her success, she was willing to take a chance on finding her own path to happiness.

Wilma had finally stepped out of the nest. There were still some twists and turns ahead for her, as she would soon begin to wrestle again with the bigger questions. But for now, it was enough to know that she was alive, that life was still beautiful, and that for today, she could breathe in the fresh air, and be grateful for her freedom.

And what had been happening to Dick, in these six or so years since Wilma had first fallen ill? At first, when he returned to Loveland, he had been horrified by the state of things. His children had been left alone to commit their mother to a mental hospital. The farm was all right, but was in disarray, after nearly a year of deferred maintenance. His daughters were somewhat friendly, but mostly were relieved that there was someone there again to take care of things. They didn't talk to him much, and he didn't ask questions. He was vaguely aware that that they were doing well academically, but he had never really been involved in their choices. When his youngest told him that she had decided to become a missionary, he rejoiced inside. This was his much cherished dream, which he had never shared with his family. He had never told them about the real reason for his east coast trip. He rightly assumed that this would have infuriated them, and selfishly, he also did not want to face someone making light of his visions nor his quest to serve the Lord.

Things with his son were not so good. He had never really known how to talk to the boy, and now Mike was interested in all this eastern religion, which was just plain wrong, from the Lord's point of view. And since religion was simultaneously both his and his son's favorite interest, there was not too far to go in conversation without hitting a land mine. He had also missed his son's entire senior year of basketball season, basically missed his time in the limelight. Though Mike didn't say anything, he imagined there was some resentment there.

He had never really been close to his eldest daughter. It seemed they were always at loggerheads, for some reason or another. But it was easier when she returned to Colorado, with the grandkids. They were a ray of sunshine in his life, a pure pleasure. They loved the farm and the pets, which somehow kept producing puppies and kittens periodically, which were no end of entertainment for the kids.

So Dick did what he did best. He withdrew, and did what life asked of him, occasionally popping his head out of his "rabbit hole" to have a look around. He continued to read his bible daily, maintained the farm, and he took an outside job supervising construction, to help the family make ends meet. He was inseparable from his dog, who rode shotgun with him in the front seat, everywhere he went. He talked to him regularly, fed him scraps from the table, and basically lavished him with all the affection he did not know how to show his children. It was not missed on his observant daughters, who once or twice dropped a caustic comment about how he spent more time with his dogs than he did with them. He oftentimes had trouble sleeping at night, and would listen to Art Bell, a nightime radio host, for hours in the pitch black, talking about aliens and conspiracy theories. This was his lifeline to the outside world, you might say. His bedroom was now the room his son vacated when he graduated high school. And secretly, Dick was penning his own book, which he kept in a metal lockbox under his bed. It was the story of his miraculous conversion, and of his call to serve the people of Russia as a missionary. It was the story of the significance of his human life.

He felt sorry for Wilma. It might be a stretch to say that Dick felt guilty for what had happened to her. He thought most of it was her own doing. His choices still seemed logical to him, and you might say that Dick had a few problems with empathy. He had spent so much of his life learning ways to tune people out, that even when he wanted to understand, he simply was unable to see what people were really getting at, most of the time. So the easiest thing was to read, listen to his shows, pet the dog, and do what was required. His life was uncomplicated, and was happy, after a fashion. Dick didn't expect to feel intimacy with anyone, so he didn't miss the absence of that with his family.

When Wilma announced that she would be moving to Estes Park, he wasn't particularly surprised. She had been threatening divorce for years, and probably would have done it, had it not been for the mental illness. He was not sure she would be able to go it alone, but he thought it was game of her to try. She was a tough old broad, and he respected her for that. The farm would still be here for her if she decided to return, or had to return.

P'oesay Apyan:

Things were not going well for my people now. We had moved far back up in the mountains now, and the winters were very harsh. Sometimes, our babies would get a cough, and would not make it through the winter. But the valleys were no longer available to us. Fort Logan had spread and grown into a big city now, and was a major stopping point for all those rivers of Ant People who headed toward the setting sun, in a seemingly endless stream.

But the worst part was that even the mountains were no longer a safe refuge for us. We had found a few open mountain valleys with rivers and lakes, and we had discovered that the mountains possessed large deer with rounded horns, and these brothers had kept us alive during the long winter months. The white men only crossed our mountains in the summer months, on their way to the Great Waters, where the stories of gold and silver were becoming more and more common. Sadly, our red brothers told us tales of our own people, the red men, becoming obsessed with the gold and silver. And, seduced by the spirit water of the white men, they had lost their souls and lived in the white men's encampments, and taught them the red man ways, which were then being used to capture the red men and use them as servants. We heard worse, too, of senseless slaughter of the red men who dared to defy the white men's wishes. These stories shocked us to the core. It was as if a poison had arrived on the land, and was spreading and slowly killing our future.

But at least up until now they had no interest in the high mountains, with their storms and snow and cold weather. The mountains here were far too rocky to attract the farmers in the valley. So we had our refuge.

But then we heard the worst news of all. Gold had been discovered in our mountains, in a place which was not far from where we lived. Now the hordes of hungry and angry white men were headed straight for our mountains. Once again we had to say goodbye, this time to our big-horned deer and our mountain valleys, and move to the south. We discovered drier country there, but at least there were fewer settlers, and they were of a different type. They brought big cows that grazed on the dry, yellow grass that covered these valleys, and put up thin metal strands to keep their animals from wandering as they waited for slaughter. These thin strands were no obstacle to the red men, and the meat was good, so at first we enjoyed hunting these creatures, though it was odd to be taking an animal that did not run. But we discovered that even though only a few Ant People would possess many, many cattle, and far too many to feed one family, they did not want to share even one cow of their plenty with the red man. We were shot at, and eventually hunted, too, and so we were driven back into the mountains, which were now crawling with the white men, thirsty for gold, and violent with the spirit water in their veins. It seemed there was nowhere to turn.

I spent many quiet hours with earth Mother, seeking her direction. Our elders were old and tired now, and it seemed that all the movement had disconnected them from their own Spirit source. My wife turned her sweet eyes upon me for direction, and my sons stood ready to do as they were bidden. Others in the tribe were becoming restless, and there was talk that I was "weak" and unable to lead. There was talk of finding a new Chief to lead our people. I waited to see what would take place, willing to step down if Mother wished this. But the emissaries kept coming to me, seeking advice, and bringing me news of the fate of the red man in other districts. It was breaking my heart to hear the tales, and many of them I did not share with my tribe. It was hard enough for us to muster enthusiasm for the hunt these days, without also having to hear about our brethren being dismembered and beheaded, to be paraded on sticks in drunken orgies, or families of red people, men, women and children, being herded like cattle into large wooden pens, and then shot and left for the vultures.

Why was Mother permitting such senseless killing? Why didn't she wave her powerful hand, and wipe away the white men with a big flood, and leave us on the shores of a new Great Waters, in peace again? And what was to be the fate of Mother herself, if the white men continued in their path of destruction? I heard now that they were mining to the north of us, digging big holes in the mountains, and poisoning the rivers and the fish with stinking, yellow waters. Was there no end to the evils that the white men could do?

I will admit that I too was becoming tired. I had not yet reached 50 years, but I felt that my life was long and had been filled with hardship. I was grateful that I had lost only one child in my life, and this one was not lost to the white man, but to natural causes. But my heart wept for the losses of so many others. Most disturbing to me were the tales of the red men who were becoming addicted to the spirit water, who would then go out and take white women in exchange for trinkets, and even raise their hands to beat their wives.

Finally, I decided that I needed to go and speak with the white men. There were some now who could serve as translators. It was not hard to make contact. All we had to do was form a delegation, and walk into the nearest settlement, in our fanciest ceremonial costumes. It was clear in that way to all who saw us that we were there on official business, and not just to drink the spirits and fight with the white men.

On my first visit, we were unable to speak to anyone about our dilemma. We were told that a message would be sent to the nearest fort, and that an emissary would come to meet us in one week's time. This was fine with me. I was still not sure what I wanted to say to this representative of such an evil force. What would he be like? Would he simply lift his fire stick and kill me, assuming that I was a great leader, and that it would be easier thus to conquer my people? With this in mind, I sent a message to the village we had entered, through our translator, to make it clear that we came in peace, and asked protection for a peaceful meeting. I also hinted that that I represented many red men, and that we would continue to cooperate with the white man, if our delegation was left in peace. The message did not directly insult or threaten, but seemed to suggest that if provoked, we might fight back. While it was true that the red men for the most part had been overpowered by the white men, there were stories of successful insurrections, in which entire villages of white men were burned to the ground. Fire was our only real weapon against them. While these burnings rarely created any deaths, they were very costly the white men and we knew that they did not want trouble any more than we did.

So in one week's time, I had my meeting. In the end, it was very uneventful. I was led into a cave-like structure with strangely angled walls that made me feel uncomfortable and disconnected from Mother. But I quietly observed carefully the man opposite me. I looked in his face, and I saw that the pupils were narrow within his light colored eyes. I could smell on him that he felt fear of me, and I realized that I was as unfamiliar to him as he was to me. He was decorated with many colored ribbons on his chest and arm, and wore a headpiece which he removed when I entered the room. I also removed my headpiece, assuming that this was a custom of his people. He made a gesture toward a chair, and I bowed. He paused for a moment, and then sat on a chair opposite the one he had gestured toward. I realized that he had invited me to sit, and I sat.

Then, as is the custom with my people, I began to stare at him, to get to know him before we spoke. I saw that he was not far from me in age, but his skin was very pale, as if Mother had not touched him with her hand to give him the warm tone of earth when he was born. It briefly crossed my mind to wonder how the white men were born, and where they had come from. Surely they were born of their mothers, like us, but perhaps they did not come from Earth Mother? Perhaps they were children of the Sky, and this was why we were at war with them, and why they did not know how to respect Mother. I made a note to ask my translator later if he had heard any stories of the origins of the white men.

The white man began to speak, in quiet respectful tones. My translator remained silent, as he continued. But as he spoke, his pitch became more insistent, and when he finished, he finished with a flourish of anger, and he stood up. I looked at him in puzzlement, and then looked to my translator, who also looked puzzled.

My translator stated, "The white man says that he is glad that you have finally come to him to beg his forgiveness for the crimes against his people. He appreciates this gesture of peace, and will make it easier for you when the settlement programs are begun to the south. But he says that he and his people are tired of the red men standing in the way of their progress, and that we will have to leave these mountains. These mountains have been claimed by some government, which is in a place called 'Washington' and there was a document signed by the red people, saying that they will leave all of this land for the white man now."

This message was very startling for me. What was this document? My people had signed nothing. Did the white men think that all red men were alike, all members of the same tribe? Suddenly, I was struck with the vastness of the ignorance I was facing. I looked with pity into those cold eyes with their tiny pupils, which saw nothing. I looked long and hard, wondering if he would be able to see me, but his eyes remained blind.

I stood up to leave, and bowed to him respectfully. As I turned, he interrupted, a look of confusion on his face. I think he had expected something more momentous than my silence. He stated something quickly to my translator, who turned to me and said, "The white man wishes for you to speak something in response to his comment."

I turned and looked at him again, and for a moment I could see into his eyes and into his soul, and I realized that he was asking me for guidance, for understanding of what was taking place. So I returned to my seat, and sat down again. I asked the translator to sit comfortably, and I began my tale.

I told the white man how I was raised in the valleys and plains, where we hunted deer and harvested grain. I told him how we had watched from the trees, as the first white men had built their first fort, nearly 40 years before. I told him how the screaming of the trees had originally led us to the white men, but now we were used to the screams, and no longer heard them. I told him how I was raised by many mothers and fathers, since my own parents had both been lost when I was young, and as a result, I had become very good at seeing the world through the eyes of all my people, and as a result, I had become a great Chief.

I told him that my people suffered now, because we had to leave the warm plains, and move to the cold mountains, and that often our babies died of the cough in the long winters. I told him that the white men had now come to our mountains and were now poisoning our rivers. I told him that many of my people had sent emissaries to me from tribes far away, who told me of tales of slaughter and sadness, and that I attempted to keep these sad tales from the ears of my people, who were already discouraged.

I finished my long tale with my hands open and face up on my knees, which was a gesture of asking for assistance among my people. I said, "So now I come to you, and hear a tale of a new 'settlement' and an agreement which I have not heard about. Now you speak to me with anger. Here is my question to you. What would you have me do? What message would you have me bring back to my people?"

At first, the white man was silent. While I had been talking, he had listened carefully, his eyes trained on my face, and I saw that slowly, the pupils were opening wider, the smell of fear was gone, and he was beginning to hear my words. When I asked my final question, he cast his eyes down, and I saw his shoulders stoop slightly in defeat.

When he looked up at me, I saw that his eyes had filled with tears, and there was another look in them, and that look was unmistakably pity. This shocked me more than anything else that I had seen or heard on that day. In that instant, I knew that things would not go well for my people, and that I would have no good news to bring to them on this day.

His words were simple and noncommittal. He said, through my translator, "I will take your question to my superiors, and will have an answer for you in a fortnight."

We stood again, this time together, and he walked by my side to the door as I left. I understood this to be his way of showing me respect, and as I left, he bowed slightly to me, in imitation of my bow to him. This might have made me happy, had this been a normal meeting between chiefs of warring tribes. But now I knew that the man I had spoken to was no chief. He was as helpless as I was to stop the killing and desecration of our mountains. While he told me nothing, he told me all that I needed to know. I returned to the tribe in silence, pondering what would come next for my people.

~~~ ∫∫ ~~~

CHAPTER TEN: THE TEST OF THE SILVER WAY

≈≈≈≈≈≈≈≈≈≈≈≈≈≈≈≈≈≈≈≈≈≈≈≈≈

Wilma's Story:

There was only one little problem in my plan to launch a new life in Estes Park. The work there was only seasonal. By October, the whole place was boarded up for winter, and only a few restaurants stayed open through the winter months. Most of the traffic through Estes Park passed over Trail Ridge and on to Grand Junction or Granby, or round about to Aspen. And since Trail Ridge was usually closed by the end of October, due to snow, the stream of visitors became a trickle, and then virtually dried up.

My office was shutting down in mid-September. It had been a glorious summer, and I offered to keep the office open for free until October 1, since my lease was up then. My bosses agreed, so I had two final sweet weeks in Estes Park to see the place wind down, before I turned the key in the lock a final time, packed up my suitcases and headed back to Loveland.

It was funny that the farm was the same....exactly the same as when I had left it. I hung my clothes back in the closet in the open gap that I had left when I took them. The smells were the same; the dogs licked me the same way, the kitchen cabinets still squeaked in exactly the same places. But somehow, it was all different now. I felt bigger.

It was a nice "bigger." I felt more expansive, more confident. I didn't quibble with Dick anymore. Oddly, I felt a little sorry for him, there in his room with his earphones stuck in his ears, piping in his classical music and his talk shows, all day, every day. I found myself gravitating to the outdoors more now. I went out and saw how the poplars were turning that beautiful golden and orange, with accents of light green, looking like flames licking the sky in the evening sun. The farm had four wonderful trees, among its smaller, less significant ones. Two were tall---very tall---poplars. One stood due east of the house, right outside the dining room window. The other was just outside the back door, centered on the side of our little yard, facing the corral. Both trees were probably 4 or 5 stories tall, and towered above everything else on the farm, including the big red barn. Our other tremendous trees were both willows. They had broad strong branches that reached out wide, and had tendrils of small branches that fell back toward the ground with small, tear-shaped willow leaves that also faced down toward earth. These were known as weeping willows, because every branch had these downward facing tendrils, like tears reaching for the earth.

The willow in front of the house had a big lilac bush as its companion, and in the spring, the bush was colored solid lavender with blossoms, and their scent was heavenly. When we arrived home at night, that scent would hit us as soon as we opened the car door. The willows were both home to tree forts, which Dick had helped the kids build when they were little. Mike and the girls would give me a heart attack when I saw them hanging off the edge of the fort by their hands, before they dropped another body length to the ground beneath them, rolled on the grass, and came up grinning. Wasn't that what we had gotten the farm for? So that our kids could grow up strong, take risks, get some confidence? Wasn't that what we had needed the farm for, too, Dick and me?

I wondered, what our lives would have been like if Dick had not been kicked out of the FBI, and we had continued to be rotated every two years to a new city, our kids having to learn a new school system and develop a new set of friends? Would we have tired of the bridge games and the petty office politics eventually, anyway? When it was all falling apart, back in Grand Forks, I had felt like my dream was dissolving. All I had ever wanted was to be a good housewife with a brood of kids, wearing an apron and making cookies. I had been a Girl Scout leader for Shannon when she was a brownie girl scout, and had taken the girls on outings, made signs for bake sales, dressed up for costume parties. Mike would ride his bike down the block to the neighbors, and then come screeching to a halt in front of our wide front porch, and bound into the house to get something to drink, leaving the bike all askew. My little darlings had their fluffs of curly blonde hair, and were always giggling about something. Wasn't this what being a family was all about? About being "normal," and living the American dream?

Then Dick had decided to take on J. Edgar Hoover, and there was that crazy period when he was checked into a mental hospital himself, and then released from duty, to sit brooding in a dark corner of the living room for days on end. In a moment, light had turned to darkness.

But thinking back on it now, as I sat in my lawn chair with a dog under one hand and a drink in the other, facing that line of deep blue peaks in the distance, and watching the riot of color that was a Colorado sunset, I realized that I would have traded all of those years in North Dakota for one of these sunsets. I took a deep sigh and let my head fall back and my eyes close for a moment. I realized that I felt very, very still. I could hear the trees rustling about me, and a bird or two chirping. In the distance was the soft roar of Highway 287, passing by the end of our two-block long driveway. I remembered watching the girls when they were little, putting on their white rubber boots and mittens and gloves, and slipping and sliding up that driveway to wait for the bus at the top every school-day morning. I thought of the parade of puppies and kittens that had played in that back yard, and frolicked through the house. I remembered the day I discovered that the girls had taken an entire litter of bunnies out of the rabbit hutch, and had hidden them in their closet upstairs. They had looked so cute in there that I had let them stay for days, until all the girls' shoes starting filling with pellets and smelling of rabbit urine, and I made them take them outside again. I thought about the day that Shannon blew the whistle on Mike's distillery operation in the attic of the garage when they were teens, where he was producing gallons of wine. She also unveiled an ingenious trap door he had cut under the carpet in his floor, where he was brewing beer. I thought it was enterprising, and I wanted to congratulate him. But of course we had to throw all that perfectly good wine and beer out. This place was so full of memories.....

So what if Dick had not gotten kicked out of the FBI? I think a little part of each of us would have died. Or perhaps it would be more accurate to say that a big part of us would never have been born. I thought of Dick back then, clean shaven, in a suit and tie with a white shirt, every single day. Even when we went out with friends, that shirt and tie were always in place. He had worn cufflinks back then, and I was always in heels. My closet was still filled with the many colored high heels from those days, and the back row of the closet was filled with party dresses that I never wore now. These days, Dick was easily 20 pounds heavier, and he sported a bushy beard. He had a big barrel chest, and strong arms and hands, and his jeans were always sliding a little below his belly. His shoes were nearly always work boots, just as mine were always comfortable flats. I liked Dick much better this way. And I liked me much better this way, too.

When the kids were little, and we would sometimes take a drive to Denver, 60 miles away, to visit the zoo, or go shopping, we would whizz past these brand new developments along the highway. As they say, these were houses that, "if you've seen one, you've seen them all." A little ditty came to my mind from somewhere in my past and I taught it to the kids. "Little boxes, on the hillside, and they're all made out of ticky-tacky, and they're all made just the same." After a few trips, they would spontaneously start singing that song, every time those rows of houses appeared along the road. We could have ended up in one of those houses, or in an endless string of houses just like those. But instead, we had found this little postage stamp of land in the midst of a wide plain, our little oasis among the checkerboard of fields around us, and we had painted it and fenced it and populated it with animals, and we had made it our own, a unique expression of our tastes. I realized that, for all our differences, Dick and I really weren't that far apart. This place suited us, to a tee.

And just as I realized this, I realized that I wanted to leave.

What had happened was that I had grown bigger somehow. This farm was like the mother that I came home to, to get one final hug, before I went out to face the world again. I had now had my own taste of adventure, and I wanted more. I went out to look for an apartment to rent in Loveland. I wanted to be around people again. I wanted to live someplace where I could walk to the store, or to the park. I settled on a little apartment not too far from Lake Loveland. I had to get in a car to go most places, but then this was Loveland, not Estes Park. This place was bigger than my apartment in Estes Park. It had two bedrooms. The whole place had wall to wall carpet, which wasn't my favorite, and it smelled a little new to me, but I could get used to it. Before I could change my mind, I had moved in.

This time, I was able to take some things from the farm with me. I chose the "hutch," which was my Canadian name for the big wood display piece where you set up all your fancy dishes and silver spoons, for the world to look at. Back at the farm, our hutch got somewhat dwarfed by the big black wood burning stove, our giant dining room table which seated eight, but normally had the leaves down, and the piano, all crammed into a perhaps 12 x 15 dark paneled room. But here in my new apartment, with its white walls, the hutch shone like a star, and I took out my silver polish and really made those silver spoons shine like no tomorrow. We had purchased them on our vacations, back in our traveling days, and I had a spoon for most of the places we had lived. There was one for Washington D.C., and one for Salt Lake City, another for Minneapolis, and one for Yellowstone. I loved them. They were a bit of refinement that meant something to me, and I liked having them with me.

I also took the sofa, in a fit of rebellion. I realized that it would leave a big hole in our giant living room, back at the farm, but I had picked it out, gosh darn it, and I wanted to have it with me. Dick hardly put up a squabble, and even helped me move. I think he had become accustomed to farm life without me, and he always sat in his lazy-boy chair by the fireplace anyway, so it wasn't like he would be left without options.

It was fun decorating my new house. I found an old panel I had painted years before for the kids, full of wild animals, that had been shunted off into a corner of the living room, and gave it a prominent place, and even dug out my old oil paints, and resolved to start painting again. The best part was bringing Shannon over to show her my new digs. I was surprised that her first concern was for the expense. She didn't seem to understand how important it was for me to continue in this experiment of living free of the shackles of the past.

Of course, I brought those ever-present little pills with me also. In all the excitement, I did forget to take them for a couple of days, but then I remembered, and got right back on track. It did occur to me that it would have been nice to have someone around to remind me, just in case. But I didn't want to ask for help these days. This experiment was not about that.

The days passed happily, and I did pick up a little part time work in the neighborhood, doing some typing. I couldn't wait until Christmas, when both Kelley and Erin had promised to come home. Look at me! My kids had left the nest, and I had flown out with them!

They came for Christmas, as planned, and it was a great one. Erin was looking older, and quite happy. He face was cleared up, and she was positively glowing. She had even found a boyfriend, among her missionaries in training, and was enjoying her stay in Florida. Kelley had landed a job quickly with the Polytechnic Institute of New York, in the department of transportation planning, through her connections from the California conference, of all things. And then she had lost it, just as quickly, and had been working as a waitress in an Italian coffee shop, before she quit that job to come home for the holidays. Mike arrived from Denver with his girlfriend, and Shannon and Grant and their kids were present, so we had a full house!

I even persuaded them to celebrate Christmas at my new apartment, and invited Dick along for the ride. He of course brought the dogs, and the celebration was complete! I felt like we were back to normal, a family again. All it had taken was me finding me again. It was fun. The laughter was abundant, and I couldn't get enough of hugging everyone. We made hot chocolate, played cards a little, and talked and talked about everything that was going on.

When the kids were growing up, I had created a few Christmas traditions. One was that we would always open only one present on Christmas Eve, and the rest would be left for Christmas day. I always went overboard at Christmas, and there would be dozens of presents under the tree, most of them for the four kids, of course. But if you figured that each of us had to buy for everyone else, then that was six times five is 30 gifts to start, and I often couldn't stop with only one gift per kid. So one gift on Christmas Eve didn't make a dent in things, and I always got to pick it. And the gift was always pajamas. That way, we all got to put on the pajamas and parade around in them, and then go to bed in our Christmas pajamas.

Well, apparently, my kids remembered the tradition, because when I opened my Christmas Eve gift, it was a fluffy baby blue floor length nightgown, with frilly white ribbon around the baby doll panel in the front. There were a couple of startled glances as I pulled it out for a closer look, and one of them was mine. Then Erin said, with a smile, "Here, Kelley, open yours!" She did, and much to her surprise, Kelley pulled out the identical blue nightgown! But we weren't finished yet. I handed Erin her box, and said, "Take a guess!" She opened it to find the identical baby blue nightgown again! Of course, we immediately put on our three nightgowns, all bought at different times and even in different towns, and had our pictures taken together, arm in arm. What a magical night that was!

I fell asleep late that night, in my own bed in my own apartment, and slept very soundly. Who knew what tomorrow would bring, but for now, life was very, very good. And the truth was that it was worth all the effort, to feel what I felt tonight.

~~~ ∬ ~~~

Wilma was not the only one who was relieved that Christmas. The strain of the previous years had taken a toll on all the family. Mike had managed to distance himself, and perhaps had fared the best, but it had been very painful to see his mother under those inhumane conditions. Kelley and Erin had been embarrassed more than once, when their manic mother had managed to get out and about, and done some strange and difficult to explain behaviors in public places. And of course, their biggest loss had been their mother's nurturing, at a time when they really could have used some direction. Shannon had perhaps the most sensitive soul of all, and cried to see her mother going through such ups and downs. In deciding to return to Colorado from Oregon, a place she had really enjoyed, she had partly factored in the fact that she would be closer to Mom, and could perhaps help her stay steady. She also thought it would help for her kids to be close to their grandmother. She had been shocked to see the condition Mom was often in, so this latest change was a welcome relief. And Dick, of course, had been forced to put all his travel plans on hold over these years, and though the book manuscript under his bed was growing steadily these days, it would be nice to be able to hit the road again, if only for a short trip, here or there.

Overall, this Christmas was like the feeling after a thunderstorm that has darkened the skies, and then washed away all the soot and dirt with the rain, and left you with fresh clean air to breathe in deeply. Everyone slept well that Christmas night.

P'oesay Apyan:

I had only a half a moon's time to figure out what to do, what to tell my people. I thought back to those years, long ago, before the white men had appeared on our land, and I realized that not only Mother had lost. We too had lost something. I had told the white man that we no longer heard the screams of the tree mothers as they were chopped down. I had just sat in a tomb composed of rotted trees, in the white man's village, and my body had not even registered the death around me. We had become desensitized.

I realized that there is something that happens when a person experiences pain again and again, in repeating patterns. At first there is pain, and when it occurs again, the pain feels worse. Then after a while, we feel it less and less, until a terrible moment happens when we no longer feel it at all. Unfortunately, when we reach that point, our soul has fallen asleep. I realized in one horrible moment that I, the Chief of my people, had fallen asleep. I was not fit to lead my people, until I could again hear the cries of the earth.

Instead of returning to the village, I turned to the forest. I was sure that the news of our visit had already reached the tribe. They would be looking to me to interpret the white man's words for them, and I was not yet prepared to do that. I walked deep into the forest, and I sat under a tree. I was reminded of the day of my mother's death, so many years ago. On that day, I had cried also, and had reached out to Mother, in my sorrow. My tree mother had cradled me, and I had slept against the sharp bark of her skin. I had realized that day that Mother was always there, all around me, always cradling me, though our earthly companions would come and go. Mother would never leave me, and I would never leave Mother. It was impossible to ever leave her embrace, for she was all around me. And when my life left me, my ashes would return to Mother, to feed another life after me. In this way, no life was ever lost, and we were never separated from Mother.

Just as I had on that day those long years ago, I allowed myself to cry into the strong bark of my tree mother. I cried with my arm stretched around her trunk, until all the tears had been spent, and had watered the ground beneath me. And as those tears fell, I felt my spirit being renewed. I could not say that I was born again, since I was still here with my tree mother, and nothing had changed outside of me. But inside, my spirit remembered. I knew that I was a child of Mother, and that nothing, and no white man, and no tragedy of my people could ever change that for me.

I knew then that the strength of my people would never rest in the fire power. Fire power was the sign of weakness, of a closed heart, of eyes that could not see. We were the people of the many eyes, and we could see all of our earth, all of the beauty of the earth around us. We were the people with vision, and suffering would not bring us blindness, but greater light. And eventually, our light would shine even upon the white man.

Perhaps it was our destiny to suffer. But this also was our destiny---to see with our many eyes, and to cure the blindness of others. I had seen into the white man's eyes. I had seen that in one afternoon, my stories had brought him from blindness to sight. If it had happened with him, it could happen with others. Mother was laughing with me again, in the sounds of the birds, and in the babbling of the stream, not far away. I looked up, and saw the dappled green and gold of the light sifting through the trees above my head. I remembered that life contains both darkness and light, and in that moment, I remembered to embrace the darkness, together with the light. Our path was not to resist change, nor to resist darkness. Our path was to embrace both the darkness and light that make up our lives, and to look up to the sky above, and feel the earth beneath our feet, and give thanks to Mother for the gift of life that all of us carry, from the smallest to the tallest, and from the red man with his spear to the white man with his fire power.

I listened again to the sound of the brook moving over the rocks, as it made its way down the mountain. I realized that the moving waters had the greatest freedom. No obstacle could stop the moving waters, as they made their way to the plains to feed the thirsty soil. When an obstacle appeared before them, the moving waters simply moved around it, or picked the obstacle up and carried it on their strong backs, as they continued their race to the plains. My people were the Moving Waters. And that day I took a new name for myself. I was now Chief P'Oesay Apyan. I was Chief Moving Waters.

In that moment, I understood that there was nothing to fear. We were all in the arms of Mother, and Mother could not abandon us. We were one with her, and we were one with each other. Yes, there would be change. The white men had come, and they were testing Mother, just as they were testing us. We had found ourselves caught between the mind of the day and the mind of the night, and, with Mother, we now were facing the Test of the Silver Way. And this Test would give us the great gift that was always its promise: the gift of wisdom. And for the red man, there is no greater gift than the gift of wisdom.

~~~ ∫∫ ~~~

CHAPTER ELEVEN:

MOVING WATERS

≈≈≈≈≈≈≈≈≈≈≈≈≈≈≈≈≈≈≈≈

Wilma's story:

Christmas ended, and everyone went back. Mike to Denver, Dick to the farm, Erin to Florida, Kelley to New York, and Shannon and family to their little house in the foothills above Horsetooth Reservoir. And I sat in my little apartment, starting to get bored. It was good. I felt so free, and I guess I could say I felt---stable. Strong. I felt strong. And that was a good thing.

But the truth was that the money was tight. By April, Kelley had decided that NYC was too much for her, and had gone to visit Erin in Florida, and was sleeping on the beach. Then she decided to come to Denver and work with Mike doing construction, because he had a crew and could use the help. It turned out that Kelley had returned to NYC, abandoned waitressing, and had taken up drywall finishing, and liked working with her hands! So now two of my little geniuses were working with their hands, and even Erin had been learning and doing construction in her missionary work. Considering their 95% plus scores on aptitude tests all through school, this was ironic to me. Though by the same token, there was Dick, with his business degree, an ex-Air Force officer and FBI agent, supervising sheet metal construction. Life threw us some curve balls, that was sure.

So by the time Kelley had made it back to Colorado, I was back in the farm again. It was like my comfortable old pair of shoes, and it sure was much easier to meet expenses from there. Before the end of that year, both Kelley and Mike had decided to move to Miami, Florida, following their guru, to whom Kelley also now subscribed. Shannon, Dick and Erin were still fundamentalist, and I was still somewhere on the fence, I guess watching it all. Before Erin shipped off to Scotland, she decided to get married, and came back to Colorado for a whirlwind ceremony to a white-blonde man with baby-blue eyes that none of us knew. At 19, she was definitely the youngest Roark to get married. I wished them well, but had my trepidations.

The next years went by, more or less like the previous ones. I would go a year or two without an incident, and then I would find myself back in the hospital again. We sampled hospitals all up and down the "Front Range," which is what they call the line of mountains that run north and south through the middle of Colorado, adjacent to the flatlands. I even stayed a few weeks once in Pueblo, at the State Mental Hospital. I could write a book about all the various ways that hospitals have found to control and dehumanize patients. But over the years, there were some good ones, along with the bad.

On the bad side, there was the psychiatrist I was ushered into for the first time. Trying to begin a conversation, I asked him if he wanted to talk to me about my problems. Without looking up, he simply barked, "Oh, your problem is just chemical," and pushed a prescription over the desk at me. I sat there a moment, thinking of the jobs and self-esteem I had lost, the trauma of the hospitalizations, the weight gain and nervous ticks that were increasing with the years, and the fact that I was pretty much useless to my family these days. Then I shrugged and got up, saying over my shoulder as I left, "Yes, you are probably right. The only problems I have are chemical." I hoped he got the sarcasm, but I expect it was lost on him.

But then there were the good ones, like Dr. X. I won't give his name here, and you will understand why later. He became my favorite. The first time I met him, he asked me my name, sat next to me and looked into my face, and said, "This is pretty hard on you, isn't it, Wilma?" I met his gaze, and began to sob like a little girl. He reached over and just took my hand, and held it firmly in his and let me cry a bit, before we continued with the session. It got to the point where we would opt for that hospital if we could, just because Dr. X would be my psychiatrist.

During the times that I was not loopy, Dick and I started to travel again. After all, we had no kids at home, and eventually even the two horses died, after living over 30 years each. Even old Emily the cat died, at the ripe old age of at least 20. We used to make jokes that the farm had its own fountain of youth, because our pets seemed to last forever. But eventually, with only one big white huskie to care for, there was nothing stopping us, and both Dick and I were somewhat restless souls, so we hit the road.

We bought a van, with wood panels custom built into the interior's side walls, and shag carpet on the ceiling, for some reason. It was a true "hippy van," which fortunately looked fairly normal from the outside. On the interior wood panels, the previous owners ironically had painted the Beatles lyrics: *"Isn't it a pity, now isn't it a shame, how we break each other's hearts, and cause each other pain..."*

We put a mattress and sleeping bags in it, and it made a pretty comfortable accommodation for the road trips, and you couldn't beat the room rates or the convenience! We would just set out and drive, and when we felt like it we would pull over and sleep. We saw a lot of sunsets from the road, and almost as many sunrises. Mike and Susan stayed in Florida, and had a baby boy. Kelley moved into an "ashram" and was moved to Connecticut, after a brief stint in Europe for a few months. Erin eventually finished her missionary work in Scotland after two years, and moved to Arizona with her new husband, and had two babies. Shannon and Grant decided to get divorced, and moved down from the mountain into Fort Collins, and Shannon returned to college and went on to graduate work in philosophy, while Grant became a water quality specialist for the city up near LaPorte. I had the great pleasure of watching their kids grow up, just as I had watched my own, and the farm became a haven for them also.

And life continued. Mike started his own construction company, after becoming a manager and estimator and learning the business from the ground up, and was very successful. He and Susan split up, and he ended up with custody of his boy. Kelley left the ashram after a few years, and decided to go back and finish her degree by taking tests for credit, moved first to posh Fairfield County Connecticut, and then got back with her New York boyfriend, Bob, and moved with him to Washington D.C. to go to law school and study urban planning, her long time passion. Our trips included visits to Miami to see Mike, Connecticut to help Kelley move, and Arizona to visit Erin, and a trip to the Grand Canyon, with Shannon, the grandkids, and Kelley and Bob, who was a nature nut who worked for the EPA.

And more changes took place. Now it was Erin's turn to divorce, and move back to Colorado with her two kids. She moved to Ft. Collins eventually, and lived down the street from Shannon, and their kids had a chance to be a bunch of cousins together. After a couple of years, she remarried Rod, a quiet, gentle man as religious as she, who brought his own two tow-headed girls into the mix, and then Erin and Rod had another tow-head together. So for a while there, my life was filled with grandkids, whenever Erin or Shannon had time to bring them around.

And more changes occurred. Shannon decided to get her PhD, and moved east to teach at Villanova, then in Michigan, and eventually to teach and study at the University of Connecticut, bringing her son Eli to live with her there, and leaving Willow to finish high school with her dad, and move on to study at the University of Hartford. Now our road trips included Kelley's wedding to Bob in D.C., and another trip for her law school graduation, as well as trips to see Shannon and Mike.

These road trips were not always easy for me. Kelley's graduation, and later her wedding, were particularly stressful for me, since I had already gone wacko a couple of times from the stress of a major event. So in an abundance of caution, I would always dope myself up pretty good for these events. The good news was that I made it through without creating a scene and ending up becoming the central attraction, with a grand finale of hospitalization. The bad news was that I wasn't very good company, since I mostly would stare into space, and had started to develop a stutter and slur my words, from the nerve damage caused by the drugs and the lithium. I was very self-conscious about my speech, and about the water weight, and frankly I felt like I didn't have much to add these days. I had always been so quick-witted, kind of the "life of the party." Now I was more like the "shadow self" of the life of the party. But no matter. I was always so happy to see my children again, that it made any discomfort worthwhile. They had stopped coming to us, for the most part, so we had to go to them.

Sometimes I would go after Dick again for having left me alone, or fall into a depression because it had been so many years since he had so much as kissed me, which meant that it had been decades since *anyone* had been romantic with me. But I no longer blamed him for my illness. In fact, I no longer blamed anyone for my illness. It was just something that had become part of my life, along with the hospitals and the doctors and the endless supply of discouraged patients who were my ward companions. I don't want to suggest that any of it was easy. It was far from easy. But it was my life. That much was undeniable. All of it was my life..... The kids, the farm, the mountains, the husband, the travel, and that endless cycle of hospitalizations. I was not perfect, and maybe I wasn't even useful anymore. But at least my family accepted me as I was. It could have been a whole lot worse.

At one point during all of these years, I again approached Dick and told him I thought we should get a divorce. He simply looked up and said, "We can't afford one!" I stopped and considered that, and then burst out laughing. I realized that he was right. So I stayed put.

Then Mike had the wonderful idea of bringing me to Florida for an extended visit. I loved the idea. He had an extra bedroom he fixed up for me. His son was in high school, and it would be nice to be a family together. He was a Big Man now, not only because of his 6 foot 7 inch frame, but also because his company had grown by leaps and bounds, and he was really at the height of his game, which is an interesting analogy, in light or his early career moves on the basketball court. What he hadn't achieved in basketball, he ultimately had achieved in business, and I was so proud of him. Maybe our approach, of trusting our kids to sort out their direction for themselves, hadn't been such a bad idea, in retrospect.

I loved living in Florida. I sunbathed and wore sunhats, and lazed around. Mike's house had a beautiful kitchen with marble countertops, and after the leaky old wood-frame farmhouse with its slanted linoleum floors and cracks that kept drawing the mice in during the cold winter months, it was nice to live in marble and granite, in the lap of luxury! I lost weight, and even could fit into a size 12 suit again, and miraculously, I even found enough concentration to read a good book for the first time in years! Things were going very well, and I could see how happy Mike was to be able to give me that life with him. I realized how much he really loved me. Under that joking, always "on" exterior, he was really a "softie," a sentimentalist at heart.

There was one thing I had never done. Although I could speak French almost fluently, having studied it in school as a child, I had never been to Europe, never seen the Eiffel Tower, never wandered Paris. Mike had the great idea to take me there, with Dhayan, his son, on their next trip. For me, this would be the pinnacle of my lifetime of adventures. Europe! We began to make plans to leave in a few weeks.

~~~ ʃʃ ~~~

P'Oesay had learned that life was lived best as "moving waters," that flow over and around obstacles, rather than fighting them, until they reach their destination. And now Wilma, a century later, through the constant pain and loss of control caused by her illness and hospitalizations, had learned the same lesson. Her spirit had graduated to yet another understanding of life. She no longer judged the experiences that came her way. Of course, her life had been a sea of disappointments at one time. But now she was reconciled with her fate. She knew it was not an easy life, but it was her life, and it was enough. Perhaps it could have been lived differently, but this was the way the cards had landed, and she had learned to make the best of the hand she had been dealt. Life was still beautiful, in all its many configurations. Each of them had faced the Test of the Silver Way, and each had won that greatest gift, wisdom.

P'oesay Apyan:

I returned to the tribe, and I realized that I could see now through the many eyes of my people again. I immediately sent some of the tribe to the south, to ask about the "settlements" that the white man was providing for the red man. I asked them to go until they learned of these settlements, and then to come back to me and report. I then sent a message to the white man, through the Ant People of Ft. Garland, where we had met. I told him that I wanted to see the document, and that I was prepared to negotiate over the relocation of my people.

Within six days, some of my emissaries had already come back with the news. The white man had found land where no gold or silver could be found. This land had sand for soil, and grew needle trees instead of trees with leaves that rustled with the wind. The white men had no use for this land, so he was giving it to the red men. The white man had drawn this land on a document, marked the rivers and mountains, and then given copies to the red men, and asked them to stay inside the areas they had drawn, like a big pen for cattle. Much of the land was dry and useless. There were tribes there who knew how to live in such a place, and lived off of lizards and cactus, rodents, foxes and other desert creatures. They did not speak our language of the tongue, but they spoke our language of the heart, and they would help us. The land was ancient, and had many colors when the sun was moving below the horizon. It was nothing like the world we had come from. But that world was no longer for us. I told my tribe that we would turn our faces to the south now.

One final emissary returned after eight days. He gave me an encouraging report. He had walked long, and had walked into these mountains within the white man's map, and he had found a place for our tribe to live. There was a stream, that even in the heat of summer still had a trickle of water flowing. The trees were tall, and he had even seen some sign of deer among the pine needles. There was a steep valley that would give some protection from the winter winds. I had asked Mother to find us a home where we could live out the rest of our days, and I knew that the two eyes of this brother had found us that home.

We estimated that with the children and the old ones, the journey would take five days, if we walked from sunrise to sundown. I asked my tribe to be ready to leave in one day's time. I explained that I would stay behind to negotiate with the white man. But I wanted my tribe to already be established in their new home before the white man's fortnight had passed. If the white man, or his superiors, made a decision to double-cross and massacre my tribe, as they had so many others, I wanted to be sure that my people were far out of their reach by the time they came to look for them.

The others saw the wisdom of my decision. They quickly and quietly made their preparations, and I sensed an optimism that had been missing for a very long time. We knew we would have each other, we would remain one, and that not one life would be lost. Privately, I was not as sure that *no* life would be lost, since I would remain in Ft. Garland until they were safely away. But I would be with Mother, and all was well.

In the days after my tribe left, as I waited for the white man to return, a miraculous thing happened. Slowly, members of other tribes began to emerge from the trees and cross our clearing, check our fires' ashes, and look for me to direct them to this new home in the south. Somehow, in the way that the wind spreads the seeds to the four directions to plant new lives, the news of our Exodus had spread to other tribes, also hiding in the mountains and hearing the cries of the earth. And they, hearing the call, had decided to move with us to the south. They would not wait to be herded like cattle. They would walk on their own, on their own feet, and would choose for themselves the land of their destiny.

So while my plans began with a small tribe of those I had known from birth, my tribe in the new land would be four or five times that size. I would have many, many pairs of eyes to see through! I was very grateful that I was the great Chief of all of these people, the people of the Moving Waters.

And thus I sat and I waited, as the Moving Waters flowed around me and to the south, bringing life to our new land.

~~~ ∫∫ ~~~

CHAPTER TWELVE:
THE FINAL ACT

≈ ≈ ≈ ≈ ≈ ≈ ≈ ≈ ≈ ≈ ≈ ≈ ≈

Wilma's story:

It all began well enough. It was great, actually. Mike planned an itinerary that included Italy as well as Paris. He bought me a suitcase and clothes for the trip. We traveled in style. Everywhere we went, we stayed in the nicest hotels, ate in the fanciest restaurants, and toured the world's finest museums. It was so much more fabulous than I could possibly have imagined, and here I was, finally walking the streets of Paris with my own two feet, at 64 years of age!

And I could not have hoped for a better traveling companion than my tall son and his tall son. Everywhere we went, we attracted attention because of their height, and this became funny to me. I enjoyed being a bit of a spectacle, and made the most of it. I had been stared at for much worse reasons in my day, believe me!

Mostly, I felt cared for. I knew that, though Mike had his own reasons to travel that year, this trip was all for me. I was so grateful to have a son that, in the midst of all that he was handling in his very busy life, took the time to take his old (and sick) mother on a trip to Europe. It was almost too much, to be treated so well finally in my life, and to have that treatment come from my own child, someone I had held in my arms and rocked to sleep, at a time that seemed lifetimes ago now. Life was a big circle. We were born, we struggled through the early years and the middle years, and by the final years, we were watching those we raised make their way through their own struggles, and then watching their children begin the journey for themselves. It was a cycle that never ended, and I was glad that my life had been full enough to watch three generations come to adulthood, including my own.

But traveling can be tiring, and I suspect that lithium doses can get burned up more quickly when someone is under stress. I was up and about every day, laughing, seeing new sites, and then one day, it seemed like I couldn't stop telling jokes. Everything that came out of my mouth was hilariously funny. We went to lunch at a Chinese Restaurant, and as our waiter turned away to fill our order, I told him, "Rots of Ruck, Chollie!" and burst into a fit of laughter as he bustled away in embarrassment. Mike looked mortified, but my grandson was suppressing a grin, which made me laugh more. Mike ushered us out and back to the hotel, where I set up camp and prepared to entertain myself for the night. And the next thing I knew, we were heading back to Miami again.

The airplane ride was a little uncomfortable for me. I was so restless, and seemed like everyone was working to get me to *sit down!* But eventually we landed, and it was off to races--I mean hospital-- again for me. This was Miami, so hospitals here were a totally new experience. I was only in the hospital a few days, just getting settled, when Mike came and told me that he was going to ship me back to Colorado, so that I could be with Dr. X, in the hospital I liked. He said it would be better than taking my chances on the care I might get here in these Miami hospitals. I felt a big pang of disappointment when I realized what this really meant for me. It meant that my Miami life was probably over now. Mike needed to get back to work, and I would be a fifth wheel, way too much trouble, now that I was sick again. Of course, I was up for the journey. What else could I say? And off we went to the airport.

Now I will have to tell you the saddest chapter of my entire story, but this is what happened, so I have to tell it. We made it back to Colorado without incident, and I suspect that I had already slipped from the mania into the depression before we got off the plane. I guess I was tired. Maybe it was the heightened excitement of the Europe trip, followed so suddenly by a complete change of plans. My life was never really in my control, was it, even when it looked like it was? As we walked into the hospital, I saw a familiar face as we passed in the hall, and I said, disheartened, "Oh Mary, you too?" I could remember her from one of my earliest stays, 20 years before. And here we were, right back where we started. We got to my room, Mike said goodbye and left, I lay down to rest, Dr. X came in to say hello, and left, and that was all I can remember, for a long time.

The last thing that I remember before it all went blank was that I felt this pain all through my body, like the whole thing was burning, on fire. It hurt so much, and then I just blacked out. When I came to, I was in a flat bed, and I realized that I couldn't move my body. It felt so strange that I assumed I must be dreaming, and kept waiting to wake up. The burning sensation was gone, and I could hear voices, but I still couldn't open my eyes. I tried to blink, and I couldn't do that either. I tried to sleep, but then there was a loud noise right next to me, and I felt that burning sensation all through me again, as if my veins were on fire. I wanted to cry out, to stop it, whatever it was, but it seemed that I was still asleep. After a while, the noise and burning subsided, and this is when I discovered the real horror of my predicament. Someone came and gently pushed my lids open, and put drops in my eyes. As they became moisturized, a fuzzy ceiling light came into focus, and I realized that I was not dreaming. I was in a hospital, and my entire body was frozen.

Now this was much worse than when the speech had been drugged out of me, years before. Back then, I could still move my body a little. I just didn't have motor control. But this time, I literally could not even blink my own eyes. Someone would come every so often and put drops in them. I couldn't see much, but I could hear everything. It became like a bad horror film. Here I was, lying there, and hearing people talking about me, all around me, to each other. Occasionally someone would lean over and address me, say something like "Wilma, can you hear me? I am going to try to make you comfortable," and then they would adjust my bedding or something. I became vaguely aware that first Dick was there, then Shannon, Mike, Kelley, Erin, and others. They would come and go, talked to each other a lot, and occasionally would lean over and say something directly to me like, "Mom, this is Shannon. I love you. You get better now, okay?" I liked it when they did this, and it seemed like they didn't do it nearly often enough. But I felt them there, and that was a comfort.

But my mind was in so many places during those days. It was like it would go off on a romp, and I would suddenly be going all the way back to Saskatchewan, remembering my dad sitting with me in Saskatoon, by the Indian reservation, explaining to me that Saskatoon was first an Indian settlement, before the white men were there. I found myself wondering if my dad had stayed in Saskatoon when my mom left because he was connected to Saskatoon the way I was connected to the farm, and maybe the Indians were as much his family as we were. This somehow led me to my Indian moccasins and my season in Estes Park, and how at home I had felt there in the forest. I thought about my olive skin and hazel-green eyes, and remembered from the photos that my dad had the same coloring. Suddenly, in my mind, my dad and I were Indians together, and we were on a journey, and we were surrounded by all the beauty of nature as we walked quietly together. He took my hand in his, and I was a little girl again by his side, maybe six years old, but at the same time, I was also adult Wilma in my moccasins, walking along the path as I told him about the bird that had landed on my finger that day. I wanted to cry, but my eyes would produce no tears, and then I felt anger and the presence of my mother became known. My dad faded away, and there was just her, in all her anger, a wasted witch of a woman, and I hated her. I remembered raging at her when my father was taken away. I remembered hitting and hitting at her as she gently enveloped me in her big arms and controlled me. But it was like it was all happening again. I was little Wilma, 8 years old, and furious at this big mean woman who just wouldn't leave my life alone. But I was also watching. It was all so confusing. Sometimes, I would get so overwrought with the memories that I would just fall into a kind of half-sleep, to be awakened by the machine noise and the burning sensation again.

Sometimes, I would have moments of clarity, and I would hear the doctors talking. I noticed that they would always step away when they discussed my condition. I wished I could see a mirror, to see for myself how I was doing. But then another memory would take over, and Dick and I would be at Banff with the kids, all these little blondies running toward the cool water, little towheaded Mike catching his first fish, and bringing it to me with pride and a big, gap-toothed grin. I would be sitting on the ground again, with two little tumbly balls of girl squirming together on my lap, and I was laughing. Laughing and laughing and laughing....... and then it would all fade again, or I would become aware of a new voice by my bedside, and I would try to concentrate, to catch what he or she was saying.

The days wore on, and I realized now that the passing of these days was marked by that machine and the burning sensation, which happened regularly. My mind seemed to get clearer, and I wondered idly whether, with whatever they were feeding me, they were still giving me my medications...... What a thought! Death by medicine. Certainly, if there was anything that would have killed me in this life, it would have been all those damn meds. Well, if I had ever felt powerless before, it was nothing compared to the complete powerlessness of my present situation. I could not even ask someone what was wrong with me, or how long it would take for me to get well.

At one point, I thought I was dreaming, because I heard my brother Warren's voice. Then he leaned over me, and I caught him in my blurry gaze, and it was him. The same square head and square glasses. He was saying hello. He had come from Michigan to visit me! Oh no. Even with my brain not firing on all cylinders, I knew what that meant. I was dying. I hadn't seen Warren in at least 15 years, easily, and it had been over 25 years since he had come to visit us, during the first year that we had the farm. Only my imminent death would have brought him out this far from home.

He was telling me a story about a tree. It seemed that there was a very old tree in East Lansing, over 100 years old, and they were planning to cut it down for some reason. And Warren had known that tree his entire life. So he gathered together all his publicity skills as a retired newspaper editor, and he organized a protest around that tree. He and other concerned citizens formed a circle of protective arms around that tree, until the city backed down, and decided to spare it. He waved a little newspaper article in front of my nose. Well, he was my father's son, too. I briefly wondered whether Warren was an Indian too, like me and dad, before I drifted off to sleep again.....

Each of them came and said their goodbyes. Kelley put a card in front of my face, and opened it for me to read the inside, and then she read it to me. It was a Valentine's Day card from Dick. Since we had returned from Europe in January, I had been in the hospital a long time already. The card said something like, "Valentine, after all these years, I guess you are stuck with me." When I heard the message, I felt this little jolt of pain. I think it was disappointment, maybe, a recognition that Dick was the only love I had ever known, and what a sorry love it had been. And yet, he was still here, wasn't he? And I wasn't the easiest person to handle, either. But I also had felt my eyes water and wince a little, and I knew that Kelley had noticed it, because she said, "Mom, you can see, can't you? You can hear me, too!" And from that point on, she talked to me every day, and it wasn't nearly as boring as it had been before.

She explained to me that Shannon was teaching her Philosophy classes, and had to go back, but she was coming again to visit in a week or two. She said Mike had just left, but he was coming back soon, also. She said that Erin was pregnant, so she had come only one time because she didn't want to affect the baby by getting too upset, but she sent her love. She said that the noisy machine was dialysis, and it was cleaning my blood. (So *that* explained the burning sensation!)

She told me that Dad was there every day, that he drove up the one hour every morning from Loveland, but he waited in the visitor's area down the hall all day, and then drove back at night, because he figured that I would not want to see him. Dick still didn't understand much, after all these years, did he?

She said that she was lucky, because she had been laid off of her job at Price Waterhouse a couple of weeks ago, and was collecting unemployment, so she could stay until I got well. So that explained why Kelley's voice was the one I heard most often. She told me that Liz, the daughter of my old friend Jeanne, lived in Denver, and Kelley was staying with her. She said that Jeanne had even come up to see me from Loveland, and she sent her regards also.

It felt so good to finally be making sense of what was happening to me. My mind was getting clearer every day, but my body still would do nothing. All I could do was listen, and listen I did. I heard all the noises at the nurse's station. I heard the sounds when they checked my wires, and changed my bedding. I heard the sound of the gurney wheels on the tile floors. Listening became a way for me to pass the time, and oddly, it gave me a peace of sorts.

After all, I was dying. I guess I should feel some sort of peace.

The days kept passing, and it felt like I was sleeping more than I was awake. I could not feel the moisture of the drops on my eyes anymore, and I suspected that they weren't doing that now. Things were getting very, very quiet. Kelley would sit by my bed all day, but most of the time she was reading, or writing. She would periodically talk to the nurses or give me some report, apologize to me for something that had happened a long time ago. I hoped that she knew that I loved her, that they all knew that. I would hate for them to carry any guilt along in their lives on my account. If anyone should feel guilty, it was me. Look how I had failed them. They had needed me, and I had checked out. But now that was all behind us, and all that was really left was the love. And wasn't the love all there had ever been, from the beginning?

Finally, something happened. I vaguely sensed motion, and realized they were moving me. Mike was there, and he talked to me for hours, about his life, about his dreams and plans, and about how much I meant to him. I didn't think I deserved all those things he said, that I was an inspiration to him, what a remarkable woman I was, etc. etc. But it was touching, nonetheless. The hardest part was when he cried over having left me in the hospital here. He wished so much he had never flown me to Denver. Poor boy! He felt that it was somehow his fault that I was in this state! That was possibly the hardest moment of this whole ordeal, not being able to ease his mind, to be able to tell him that he didn't do it, and I didn't do it. It was just life, closing a cycle.

Dick came to see me again that night. He said that Kelley had told him he should, and he apologized if he was bothering me. First he read the bible to me, and they were some beautiful passages in the Psalms, passages I did not remember. My mind was very foggy now, but for a moment I contemplated God. I realized that all of them had such clear ideas of what God was, and I remained in the dark, after all these years. But my life had contained so much light! When I thought of those moments looking up at a sunset, or watching puppies play, or making a snowman or painting a picture, or having a bird light on your finger..... How could life be any better than that! Had I really missed something, because I didn't have a clear concept about the Man Upstairs? Didn't the bible say that heaven belonged to the children? Well, I was a child of life, and after all these years, I still felt like a child. Wouldn't God welcome me, if he had given me all of this beautiful life to enjoy?

After the bible story, Dick read me a story from a book he brought with him. The title of the story was, "Men Are So Dumb." When he told me the title, he broke down and cried. It was kind of hard to hear him cry like that. I don't think I had ever heard him cry. He was trying to talk through the tears, and in my state, I couldn't understand any of the words. But I understood the feeling. I knew that he was trying to tell me how much he had loved me, and how he had appreciated having me as his lifetime companion. And then there he was with the guilt again, apologizing for putting me in this state. It occurred to me that maybe we all believe that we are little gods ourselves, making things happen. For the second time that night, I wished I could relieve the guilt, and tell him that years ago I had realized that my illness was not anyone's fault--not even mine. But Dick composed himself, and finished reading me the story, and he seemed calm enough when he finished.

It occurred to me that they were all saying goodbye. I knew this was true when Kelley came in and leaned over me, and whispered in my ear, "Mom, Shannon just called. She is coming tomorrow morning, but she wanted me to give you a message tonight. She said I had to tell you, 'Let go to the One who loves you.'"

When I first heard it, I felt a moment of panic, and I felt my forehead wrinkle briefly. Was I dying today? And then the message touched me with a simple understanding. Of course! The One who had given me all this beautiful earth was calling me to come back to him. The gift of this life was my proof that I had been loved and cherished all along. I had looked so many places over the years for answers. In the end, the answer was simple. I was loved.

<center>~~~ ∫∫ ~~~</center>

This was the final chapter in Wilma's life. Remember at the beginning of this tale, we talked about how she had chosen a very challenging path, in order to learn some very important lessons? Her soul had carefully chosen a group of souls to bring her into this world, and to help guide her through it, so that she could find her way to an understanding about life, the true wisdom that came from the Test of the Silver Way. She had been tried by fire, and refined and refined, until she shone like pure silver and moved on with as much gained from this life as she could possibly squeeze from it.

One day, while Wilma was still up in the Intensive Care Unit, the family met downstairs in the cafeteria with Dr. X, who had requested a meeting. He said that he wanted to tell them personally the reason Wilma was there, in intensive care. With red-rimmed eyes, he carefully told them it was because he had injected her with a dose of lithium upon arrival without taking her blood levels or checking her chart. This overdose of lithium had put her into the metabolic coma that was precipitating her death.

After he left, the family discussed for five minutes whether they would want to pursue legal action against Dr. X for malpractice, and unanimously decided against it. Money would not bring back their mother, and they were pretty sure that she would not want to destroy the career of the one doctor in her twenty year history of hospitalizations who had shown her compassion. Anyway, he would undoubtedly punish himself enough for the mistake he had made, with his own guilt.

One could say that it was the injection by her good friend Dr. X that had eventually sent her to her death. But Wilma's spirit understood it differently. Death was a choice that her soul had made, after she had fulfilled the contract she had come to this earth to complete. The manner of her death was the final act, the final lesson, the final refinement of the Silver of her soul. During those weeks in the hospital room, she had completed her journey and said goodbye. Through the "good" and the "bad," through the light and the dark, she had ultimately found peace, and learned the wisdom of acceptance. She had become one of the people of the Moving Waters and she had found her way home.

P'oesay Apyan:

I waited for the white man patiently, and in a fortnight, he appeared. It was as I suspected: he did not come alone. From my perch on the side of the mountain, I could see them coming from a distance, rows of soldiers on horseback, with him taking the rear. My translator waited by my side until all the soldiers had been hidden in the fort, and then we went to approach the town.

I had once again dressed in my ceremonial attire. It seemed the best way to show my respect for the importance of this moment. I knew that Mother smiled upon me as I made my way through the village, but in my heart, I felt fear. It was because I loved my family. I knew that Mother would welcome me, if I had to leave my body today. But it was the faces of my children that were before my eyes as I walked to meet this man, perhaps my enemy, but also my brother.

We met in the same room where we had met before. Through the translator, I explained that my people were prepared to move to the settlements that the white man had prepared for them. He smiled in response, and I saw that the smile was not of genuine happiness, but more of discomfort. I looked into his eyes deeply, and I saw pain within. He was not completely blind, but at this moment, his responses would be blinded by his pain. It occurred to me that I did not know what he had experienced in the two weeks since we had last met. I wondered if he was finding himself caught between the mind of the night and mind of the day, because of some trauma that he had experienced. I felt pity for him, but also respect, knowing that he too would be blessed with the gift of wisdom, when this Test was completed.

I sat quietly for a moment and studied him. I had again instructed my translator to sit comfortably at my feet, and I was not at all sure what to expect from this meeting. I saw through the door that there were several soldiers there waiting restlessly, as if awaiting a command. I sighed. Sometimes it is very hard to witness darkness, even when we know that with it comes light, too.

He seemed to notice my sigh, and I saw his shoulders relax. It was if he had recognized that he was in the presence of an elder, and no longer had to be in charge. I sensed his openness again, as I had sensed it on our last visit.

I asked him if he had a document, to show me the location of the lands where he would like us to move. He said he did not, but that they were about 3 days to the south of here. I sighed again, but this time in relief. Our information had been correct. I said that would be acceptable, and he said that he had brought an escort, to lead us to the new territory. I gently said that this would not be necessary, since we required no guidance. The earth was our Mother, and would lead our steps.

He stiffened at this, and responded too quickly, "but you cannot possibly know where to go without guidance." I again politely insisted that it was not necessary. He then said, "I have my orders to take you and your tribe to the settlement," and I saw that his pupils were very small again, and I again noticed the smell of fear on his skin. So he had orders from his superiors, and he feared failing them.

I then said, "As you wish. Your escort can lead those of us who are left." "Left?" he responded, puzzled. I stood, turned and told him, "Come and I will show you." I knew that now was when my life might be taken, but I had no choice but to turn my back on him, and walk out through the restless soldiers. And he had no choice but to follow me.

As soon as we had left the building, I stopped and waited for him to overtake me. I then gestured for him to lead the way, in order to give him the opportunity to ask me to guide him to my tribe. In the end, we walked side by side, with the translator, with a large crowd of soldiers following behind us. As we walked toward the abandoned campsite of my tribe, I began to talk to him. I spoke to him of the love of Mother, to have given us such a wonderful creation. I explained that my people had lived on this land for many generations, and that we knew the cries of the earth, knew the smells of the earth and the animals, and we were able to see through our many eyes, as one people. I explained that we could track an animal by the smell of fear in its skin, and that humans also contained this smell. I explained that Mother is always present to protect us, and for this reason, there is no reason for fear. When I said that, I stopped for a moment and looked into his eyes. I wanted him to know that I was aware of his fear, and that Mother wanted to comfort him through my words. I saw his eyes widen first with greater fear, and then he quieted. He responded in a low voice that sometimes he is made to see things and do things that upset and sadden him.

I then explained to him about the mind of the day and mind of the night. I explained that when the spirit is silent, the mind can become filled with fear, and if the fear becomes too strong, the soul can become lost between the mind of the night and mind of the day. I explained that mother will take him through this test, if he can learn to be quiet and listen. Mother always answers our questions, if we listen to her.

He again fell silent, until we arrived at the empty campsite. I then explained that my people had left, six days before. I saw his soldiers check the campfire beds, and confirm that they were cold. He turned to me puzzled. I told him that our Mother had already told us where we should go, and that we would never be seen in these mountains again. He had my word.

He responded, through the translator, "But my orders are to take you to the new territory." I imagined that he was both relieved at not having to force women and children into a march, and confused about what he should do next. So I extended my two hands towards him, palm up, in my tribe's gesture of submission, and told him, "Then lead me."

And so it was I that arrived at my new home, escorted by a cavalry officer and thirty soldiers. It took us three days to reach the new land, and during those three days, our translator was very busy. I taught the soldier how to watch the flight of the birds, to see where the animals were among the trees. I taught him to hear a stream from a mile away, to find water. I taught him about the cycles of the moon, and how they influence the creatures of the forest, including the people. I made him laugh when I told him that our name for his people was the Ant People, and he explained that the long lines of "ants" that made their way across the plains were called "wagon trains." He explained that the white men's word for us was "savages," but the translator could not find a word in my language to translate it. When he tried to explain that a "savage" is a brute without education or control, who will hurt others without the advantage of discipline or a moral code, I responded, "Then you believe us to be as you are, 'savages'! " He looked at me in surprise, and then he roared with laughter, which startled the men behind him. "No," he explained, we view ourselves as "civilized." As we made our way through that definition, I came quietly to this conclusion: It appeared that the white men saw the red men as a reflection in a pool. They looked at us, and they saw themselves. This was the blindness that the red man was here to remove. I nodded at his words with patience, and we continued our march.

Now my story too must come to an end. When we reached the edge of the territory, of course my tribe was nowhere to be seen. But there were other "savages" there, and I merely told him that I was fine now, that I was with my family. I knew that they were not wise enough to see the differences between us and the other tribes. He had completed his task, and ridded his territory of the terrible red man, the "savage" who could not be trusted to act with discipline or a moral code. We bowed to each other, and said our goodbyes, and I moved on to my new life.

~~~ ∫∫ ~~~

Our tribe settled in the valley that our emissary had found for us. It was big enough to host 50 families, and was far from any forts or activities of the white men for many years. Eventually, the cities in the flat plateaus became bigger, and since food was scarce, our tribe began to make objects of art, and take them to the local villages to trade. When we did, we came and went as quickly as we could. We heard terrible stories of the injustices done against the red men here, also. But here there were more of us than there were of them, so there was an uneasy peace. The "church" was here, a group of white men who wanted the red men to adopt a white god. We did not know why this white god was so important to them, since he appeared to be human and not big and containing everything, like Mother. Some of our people began to attend the meetings of the white god, because they were told that there would be endless suffering for them if they did not. Others decided to adopt the white man's liquor spirits, and when they brought these back to the tribe, I insisted that they be removed. But when I was an old man, and my sons themselves were grandfathers, the young men and women no longer listened to the elders in the way that they had done before. The white men came and insisted that we learn their language, and that our children attend the white man schools, which were run by this "church." There the children's minds became confused, and we would have to work very hard to correct the misunderstandings they were gaining in the white man's school. Eventually, it became too much, and the people began to forget. But there were always some that remembered. And every tribe still had its storytellers, who preserved the stories that had been passed down from our grandfathers.

Eventually, my tale too became one more that was passed down from grandfather to father to child to grandchild. The children heard about the people of the plains, who used to hunt the deer and gather wild grains, until the white man appeared, and then spread like ants over the landscape, and drove the plains people into the mountains and then south and south, until we arrived at this, our final home.

Ours was the tale of P'Oesay Apyan, the Moving Waters, which are stronger than any obstacle they encounter, and will always find their way home to Mother.

~~~ ∫∫ ~~~

EPILOGUE

≈ ≈ ≈ ≈ ≈ ≈ ≈ ≈

When Wilma's heart finally went into cardiac arrest, 30 days after she had walked off the airplane, Mike was sitting with her in the intensive care hospital room. He quickly called Kelley and Dick, who were there within the hour. She had been moved to a private room the night before, because the nurses were trained to see when a patient like Wilma was about the check out. They wanted to give the family privacy. Shannon's plane was due in at 9 am, and it was 4 am now. Kelley called Erin, in Loveland, and told her that Mom was passing, and talked her through the process for the next hour, with the medics attempting to resuscitate Wilma, until she finally breathed her last breath. She knew that Erin needed to be there, needed to feel her own goodbye in those last minutes. Shannon arrived the next morning, crestfallen that she had not arrived in time, but grateful that her message had been delivered. Wilma had asked years before to be cremated. They held a funeral at the Episcopal Church, where the children had attended every Christmas and Easter through childhood. There were two people who were not family at the funeral. One was Jeanne Lamb Bolton, Wilma's only friend. The other was a gentleman Wilma had usually referred to as "Old Casey," who had already been old when her children were young. He had just lost his wife, and probably knew how important it was to the survivors to show one's respect. At the funeral, Kelley sang her mother's favorite hymn:

"I come to the garden alone, when the dew is still on the roses,
And the voice I hear, falling on my ear, the Son of God discloses,
And he walks with me and he talks with me, and he tells me I am his own,
And the joy we share as we tarry there, none other has ever known."

Mike got up and spoke the eulogy. He told the story of his mother's life, as best he could remember it. He mentioned that his mother was a gentle soul, with a love for life that was infectious, and that this was the greatest gift she had given her children. And he mentioned that once, when she was sitting in the mountains, a wild bird had actually flown onto his mother's extended finger.

It was a tribute she would have appreciated.

~~~ ∫∫ ~~~

P'Oesay Apyan lived to the ripe old age of 105. By the time he died, he was a small and shriveled old man, who was passed by in the square a dozen times a day, without a second's notice. He had outlived nearly everyone who had made the long trek with him from the northern country, nearly 60 years before. He had learned to hunt lizard, grow corn, and make ovens out of red earth, and he had been a source of strength for his family and tribe for many years, until others had grown up to take his place, which is as it should be.

He died in his sleep, and his tribal family carried him 17 miles to the nearest graveyard, in a small dusty town on the high plains near the highway. A tribesman who was a stone smith carved the words, "P'oesay Apyan, Moving Waters," into a simple stone tablet, which was placed at his head as his body was lowered. At that time, it was not permitted to carry a loved one into the forest, and cover his body lovingly with dried leaves, then hold hands in a great circle, and wail to the skies, and return to the village with the body left there in the leaves, to feed the earth.

But they did carry his body gently along the highway to its final resting place, and as they walked, they quietly hummed tunes they had learned from their fathers, and their fathers' fathers. And they thought lovingly of the great Chief, P'Oesay Apyan, the great Chief of the Moving Waters, who had once brought their tribe to safety in its new land, without a single soul being lost. And after they laid his body to rest, they returned home to their village, to retell the tale again to their children.

~~~ ♫♫♫ ~~~

AUTHOR'S NOTE

I wrote this book in record time. From the time that the idea was conceived to the day I wrote the final chapter, only three days short of a month had transpired, and the editing was done a week later. I owe this rapid finish to the method of delivery of the information.

I did not always believe in the existence of "spirits" from the "other side," who can communicate with us. You might say I was, and am, an open-minded skeptic. While I have meditated for years, the idea of psychics and mediumship repelled me for years. I would not have begun to tread this path, except that I started to have spontaneous "psychic" experiences around 8 years ago, and became curious. My curiosity led me eventually to explore what is known as "automatic writing," which essentially channels messages from the subconscious, or from guides. These messages have been attributed to God, to the "Higher Self," to angels, spirit guides, ascended beings..... I decided that the messages that I received were inspired, even if I couldn't confirm their source.

My exploration led me attend a session with a medium in March of 2013. During the session, he spoke to almost everyone present, delivering messages from deceased loved ones. He told me that my mother was there, and wanted to talk to me. He also said I was accompanied by a Native American guide, who had a message that he wanted me to communicate. He said that I knew his name, and that it was two words. I immediately thought of "P'oesay Apyan," the name I had placed in my telephone contacts over two and a half years before, after finding it on a gravestone.

A few days later, I attended a meditation which was led by another psychic. She told me very firmly, "Your mother wants to talk to you!" so dutifully, the next morning I sat down and asked my mother what she wanted to say, prepared to automatically write her response. What rushed out was 18 pages about my life since her death, my relationship with my siblings, some advice, and her experiences on earth and after. She concluded with a request. She wanted me to write a book, and she wanted to write it with P'oesay Apyan, who was with her. She said that I didn't need to worry about what to say; they would give me the words. And she suggested that I begin the following morning, which is what I did.

For me, the experience was remarkable. I sat at the computer, typed "CHAPTER ONE: BEGINNINGS," and the words just poured out, until the chapter was finished. Most of the time while I wrote my mother's story, I was crying. It was like I was reliving the sadness of her life again, but from her perspective, which was even sadder than mine had been. Toward the end of the book, I also cried through all of P'oesay's passages. In the end, I felt like I had been drawn through a portal of understanding, and I could never see my mother' suffering, or anyone's suffering, in the same light again. What had been only darkness for me was transformed to light, and I knew that suffering was just one of life's many gifts. Words fail me. I only hope that the stories in these pages better convey the message that I articulate so crudely here.

After I finished writing the book, I had one more step to take. I wanted to "fact-check" what I had written. With my mother's story, I had enough personal knowledge to piece together the chronologies to be sure that everything matched up.

For P'oesay Apyan, it was a different story. After all, all I had known of that person was a gravestone, and I have never been a student of Native American history. When P'oesay said he was a Plains Indian who had moved into the mountains, that sounded dubious to me, but I wrote it as I received it. When he said he witnessed the construction of one of the first forts, and then lived through the Colorado Gold Rush, I was not sure this chronology matched up either. The most difficult for me was the idea that this tribe of Plains Indians had ended up on a New Mexico reservation. I did know that there were reservations all across the Great Plains, so it made more sense to me that he and his tribe would have ended up in one of those.

So I spent the better part of two days on the internet, reading about the history of Native Americans in Colorado and the west. I was very surprised at what I learned.

There were many tribes who were pushed west and south by the migration of the white men. P'oesay had spoken of harvesting wild grain, and I discovered that the Cheyenne Indians had begun near the great lakes and had been sedentary originally, but had been pushed into North Dakota and then south by other more aggressive tribes who were being displaced by white settlers further east, and they had adopted a nomadic lifestyle. Some Cheyenne finally ended up in Colorado, where they learned to coexist with the Arapahoe, another plains nation, the Utes, who were mountain dwellers, and others. Many did in fact retreat to the mountains as the flatter prairie land was overtaken by settlers and they were driven off. And there were many bloodbaths. I also learned that the Shoshone Indians were Plains Indians that originated in Wyoming, just north of Colorado, where this story began. Some of these split off and became known as Comanches, and many Comanches eventually settled in northern New Mexico.

The history of the construction of forts in Colorado was troublesome to me. I didn't really know which part of Colorado P'oesay had lived, so I researched the whole state, and at first could only find forts that had been built around 1860 or later....too late to have been there 35 years before the Colorado Gold Rush started in 1858. I began to doubt myself as my search turned up only Bent's Fort, which was out in the plains on a river, and never had a large community grow up around it.

Then as I checked the history of Fort Collins more carefully, I discovered that there was another fort that had been built much earlier, near LaPorte, Colorado, around 1828, just for trading. A community grew up around this fort, which was located on the path to the Overland Trail which was one of the main routes to California in those days. At one time, this community was the largest settlement in the region, at the time when the Gold Rush started at Pike's Peak, to the south. Fort Collins, a military fort, was eventually built around 1864 to protect all the settlers of LaPorte from the Indians. (Ironically, Fort Collins was decommissioned in 1867, and itself became an Indian reservation up to 1871, long after P'oesay had moved south.)

So not only did the chronology fit perfectly, but I realized that this would place P'oesay's tribe within only a few miles of the farm where I grew up! The mountain parks where the tribe hunted Big Horn Sheep could have easily been part of what is now Rocky Mountain Park, next to Estes Park, where my mother stayed.

I then looked into Fort Garland, which is located in southern Colorado near the New Mexico border, and discovered that it was built in 1858, which means that it would have been there after the Gold Rush had reached its peak between 1858 and 1861, when P'oesay's tribe was left with nowhere to turn. It replaced the largest military fort in Colorado, Fort Massachusetts, and was active for years.

P'oesay repeatedly had alluded to rumors of killings and massacres. I learned that the biggest tragedy among the many injustices to the Native Americans in Colorado occurred in 1864 just 125 miles east of Pueblo, Colorado, which is only 95 miles or so from Fort Garland. It was called the Sand Creek Massacre, and I have included a description of it in the Appendix, as an example of the inhumane treatment which P'oesay's tribe escaped by moving to the south.

The military had declared peace with a Cheyenne/Arapahoe tribe led by Chief Black Kettle. Believing that they were safe under military protection, the tribe was camped at the Sand Creek, awaiting instructions on relocation (just as P'Oesay waited). A band of military men swept through at daybreak, and brutally murdered men, women and children. The chief of these people was standing by his tent flying a white flag and American flag, insisting that no one need run because they were protected, right up until his entire tribe was mowed down. Body parts were paraded as trophies, and the massacre evoked nationwide horror and shame. The timing of this massacre would have been right at the time when P'oesay's story in this book ended, around 1864. Thus, his decision to move his tribe to the south possibly averted a similar tragedy.

I had needed to find out whether it was plausible that Plains Indians would have made their way from the mountains of Colorado to the desert of the New Mexico reservations. I also needed to confirm that there was a reservation near enough to Santa Fe to be a reasonable distance from the graveyard where P'oesay was buried. Once again, I was relieved to discover that the facts of my story matched history perfectly. In fact, I found specific mention that the Cheyenne (which may have been the nation to which P'oesay's tribe belonged), had been pushed to Colorado, had learned to adapt to mountain life, and then had splintered into smaller tribes who aligned themselves with local tribes, and that some Cheyenne groups headed south, and settled in northern New Mexico with the Pueblo Indians.

Finally, I looked at the years that reservations had been established within a close radius of the graveyard, and discovered that Santa Clara Reservation, along with others, was established by act of Congress between the years 1958 and 1960. When I looked at that reservation from Google Earth's images, I found a narrow valley with a small stream in the mountains, meeting the description of P'oesay's emissary, above the flat desert plains that lead to Santa Fe. By looking at the distance map key, I was able to calculate that this valley would be around 15 to 20 miles from the small town where P'oesay's headstone can be found, which was the distance the story said that they carried him, to reach his final resting place.

After all this was done, I decided that I needed to revisit P'Oesay's gravesite, and see what I could learn of his history personally. What I learned of his famiy makes sense, in light of the description he gave at the end of the book. Research at the library and the Office of the Indian Council revealed only that there was no recent address for the Apyan family. Church records of births and deaths similarly proved fruitless, but a kind church administrator called a friend who "knows everyone," who pointed me to the house of a pueblo resident who would have been P'Oesay's grandson's grandson.

He had no knowledge of his ancestors' history, but he remembered his grandfather, who was buried in the local graveyard, and carried the name P'Oesay Apyan, but had changed his name to an anglo name in order to avoid the constant persecution that was his life in New Mexico. (This is why no records were found.) He had moved north to Colorado and evetually to Los Angeles, where he lived until he grew older and returned to the reservation. When he was an old man, his family returned also, from Northern California, to care for him. The grandson recalled his grandfather as well dressed with shiny shoes, and as a "modern man," and I noted that his grandfather's house was well-made and a bit larger than those of the neighbors. The grandson indicated that his family were not really fully accepted in the village, that they tended to be "outsiders," and kept to themselves. He said that he and his sisters were quiet professional people, didn't drink, and just stayed to themselves and lived peacefully. And though of course he was many generations from that original tribe that I described, I noticed that his strong features were very distinct from the vast majority of the Tewa Indians I met during my stay.

While I was in New Mexico, I drove up into the mountains above the several Pueblo reservations near Santa Fe. I found a long valley protected by mountains, with a stream running through it, within the distance that the book describes, which was infused with a peace and beauty that made me feel happy to imagine this as the final stage for the end of a long life. (I used a photo of that river valley as the back cover of this book.) I learned that the original reservations had been whittled away over the years, and in fact the U.S. government has continued to attempt to reduce tribal lands, even in recent times. The history of the Pueblo Indians of New Mexico, Colorado, Arizona and northern Texas appears to be as sad as the stories of those Native Americans to the north.

Was P'oesay Apyan a chief of his people, and did the events in this book actually take place? We can't really know. But at least I am comfortable that everything that was chronicled in this story was possible. And it is possible that P'oesay has finally accomplished his goal, more than a century later, of sharing his wisdoms with the "Ant People," through this book that I have just written, and you have just read.

~~~ ʃʃʃʃ ~~~

APPENDIX: THE STORY OF THE SAND CREEK MASSACRE

FROM http://www.lastoftheindependents.com/sandcreek.htm

"Black Kettle was a peace-seeking chief of a band of some 600 Southern Cheyennes and Arapahos that followed the buffalo along the Arkansas River of Colorado and Kansas. They reported to Fort Lyon and then camped on Sand Creek about 40 miles north.

Shortly afterward, Chivington led a force of about 700 men into Fort Lyon, and gave the garrison notice of his plans for an attack on the Indian encampment. Although he was informed that Black Kettle had already surrendered, Chivington pressed on with what he considered the perfect opportunity to further the cause for Indian extinction. On the morning of November 29, he led his troops, many of them drinking heavily, to Sand Creek and positioned them, along with their four howitzers, around the Indian village.

Black Kettle ever trusting raised both an American and a white flag of peace over his tepee. In response, Chivington raised his arm for the attack. Chivington wanted a victory, not prisoners, and so men, women and children were hunted down and shot.

With cannons and rifles pounding them, the Indians scattered in panic. Then the crazed soldiers charged and killed anything that moved. A few warriors managed to fight back to allow some of the tribe to escape across the stream, including Black Kettle.

The colonel was as thorough as he was heartless. An interpreter living in the village testified, "THEY WERE SCALPED, THEIR BRAINS KNOCKED OUT; THE MEN USED THEIR KNIVES, RIPPED OPEN WOMEN, CLUBBED LITTLE CHILDREN, KNOCKED THEM IN THE HEAD WITH THEIR RIFLE BUTTS, BEAT THEIR BRAINS OUT, MUTILATED THEIR BODIES IN EVERY SENSE OF THE WORD." By the end of the one-sided battle as many as 200 Indians, more than half women and children, had been killed and mutilated.

While the Sand Creek Massacre outraged easterners, it seemed to please many people in Colorado Territory. Chivington later appeared on a Denver stage where he regaled delighted audiences with his war stories and displayed 100 Indian scalps, including the pubic hairs of women.

Chivington was later denounced in a congressional investigation and forced to resign. When asked at the military inquiry why children had been killed, one of the soldiers quoted Chivington as saying, "NITS MAKE LICE." Yet the after-the-fact reprimand of the colonel meant nothing to the Indians.

As word of the massacre spread among them via refugees, Indians of the southern and northern plains stiffened in their resolve to resist white encroachment. An avenging wildfire swept the land and peace returned only after a quarter of a century."

ABOUT THE AUTHOR

Kelley Roark grew up in the plains of Colorado, 20 miles south of Fort Collins, and spent many happy hours of her childhood exploring the mountains of Northern Colorado. She travelled northern New Mexico with her family, and her last road trip with her father was to the Albuquerque Balloon Festival, accompanied by her three-year old daughter, after which the three retreated to a small cabin, which her father had built at age 80 in the dry mountains above Fort Garland.

When her father grew too old to care for the farm, it was sold, and he moved to Connecticut to live with Kelley's sister Shannon and her family. Mike has split his time between Miami and New York, and Erin has stayed in the Loveland area with her large family. Dick managed to heal his relationships with most of his children before his death, and died peacefully at 87.

Kelley's travels have led her to live up and down the eastern seaboard, landing in Miami, where she has practiced law for over 20 years, punctuated by over three years in Costa Rica, where she hopes to live again after her daughter graduates high school. She has written travel books and other nonfiction, and is now working on a book that is inspired by the genesis of this very unexpected project.

www.ingramcontent.com/pod-product-compliance
Lightning Source LLC
Chambersburg PA
CBHW051956090426
42741CB00008B/1421